COLIN OATES

ACCIDENTAL OLYMPIAN

COLIN OATES

ACCIDENTAL OLYMPIAN
A JUDO JOURNEY

HOWARD OATES

First published by Pitch Publishing, 2021

Pitch Publishing
A2 Yeoman Gate
Yeoman Way
Worthing
Sussex
BN13 3QZ
www.pitchpublishing.co.uk
info@pitchpublishing.co.uk

A CIP catalogue record is available for this book
from the British Library.

ISBN 978-1 78531 891 7

Typesetting and origination by Pitch Publishing
Printed and bound in the UK by TJ Books Limited

CONTENTS

INTRODUCTION

WHEN ANY athlete steps into the spotlight, does any spectator have any idea how they got there? It is rarely just by hours of dedicated training, miles of travel and often painful injuries. There are many other factors; fate, luck and family background.

This is the story of how a judo player emerged from a tiny village hall judo club to a world elite athlete who would go on to represent Great Britain at two Olympic Games and England at the Commonwealth Games.

Strange though it may seem, none of this would have happened had I not purchased a *Floodlight* magazine back in 1979 and found a judo club. Growing up in the swinging 60s I was lucky enough to experience pirate radio blasting out across the North Sea – the best music the world had ever heard – watch England beat West Germany 4-2 in 1966 on a black and white television to win the World Cup, and able to listen to the then fight of the century on the radio between Muhammad Ali and Henry Cooper.

It can be of little surprise that as a schoolboy I wanted to be either a footballer, rock star or a boxer; unfortunately I could not make up my mind which I preferred so I joined a football club, a boxing club and learnt to play a guitar. Well clearly it did not work out well and I did not find fame or fortune in any of those activities. I was too small to be a footballer, realised I was a brilliant guitarist so long as no one was listening and really did not take to being punched on the nose. Oddly the latter was experienced in a football match.

This kid scored a goal; for reasons only known to myself I kicked him up the butt and he flew around and broke my nose with a right-hander I should have seen coming.

My only knowledge of judo back then was from watching *The Avengers*; no, not the Marvel franchise but the British TV series with the late Honor Blackman throwing large men with her skills, so to this day I am not altogether sure what prompted me to join a judo club. In doing so it certainly meant I could and would embark upon a long journey that would see me involved in a sport for over 40 years and trek around the world with my son Colin and Jono Drane en route to the Olympic and Paralympic Games in 2016.

THE BEGINNING 1979–1994

IT IS doubtful whether any parent who takes their son or daughter to an after-school activity or sports club can envisage how it can not only change your offspring's life but can completely change a parent's too. What follows is the complete story of how a sport totally changed the direction in life of a whole family that had yet to take shape, how it affected children not yet even born.

Back in the late 70s the decision to have children was based on whether you could afford to bring up a child. Of course child benefit seems to have been about since the Stone Age but there were no working tax credits or so-called free childcare schemes. If you had a child it usually, as in our case, meant you lost a huge chunk of income (usually your wife or partner's wages) and were essentially on your own. When my wife, Denise, and I decided to start a family, that really nice man Jim Callaghan was Prime Minister.

We were in no way prepared for the Thatcher government which would rip us apart financially over the coming years with 17 per cent interest rates on mortgages and public sector wage freezes.

I was still playing table tennis in the London leagues back then having given up playing football. In the real sense it was like football gave me up. It would be nice to say an injury ended my interest, nice to say but untrue. I was simply rubbish at the sport. In modern-day football, being on the bench has a different meaning – maybe you are being rested or it is tactical. In my day it was much simpler, you had been dropped. Sometimes I did not even make the bench in the days of one substitute.

Playing table tennis (and not ping pong) kept me fit and was the last sport I was likely to be involved in, so I thought. Our team was quite good too being in the third of six divisions so it was serious stuff. I took the somewhat short-sighted view that once we started a family my social and sporting life including my table tennis would be well and truly over. I had given Denise the usual male macho speech that once the baby was born I would have little to do with it until it was about four or five years old. I would like to think that all males, not just myself, were donuts back then. In fairness we had been fed an assortment of macho movie stereotypes, and in the 70s even had to make a special effort to see our movie heroes like Clint Eastwood and Steve McQueen at the cinema as the video age was still a couple of years away. With only limited television – yes, we were blessed with not having a Channel 4 or 5 and no reality TV either – the birth of your first child meant the end of any type of social life or entertainment; you were confining yourself to a life in front of a television set with less than a handful of channels.

As a fairly active adult I had always been keen on sport but oddly I came to judo relatively late in life in 1979 at the age of

26, just after my first daughter Charlotte was born; Colin was not even a thought back then. In 1979 that special moment of only knowing if you are going to be the parents of a little boy or girl was saved until the day of the birth; somehow I still think that is the way it should be. The moment Charlotte was born I chose to ignore that suggestion that I would have nothing to do with her until she was four or five or that my sporting life was over. Do not get me wrong, like all self-respecting men I would still avoid those nappies from hell especially as they were not the disposable ones of today. I had got the avoidance tradition down to such a fine art that even 30 or so years later and with disposable ones I can still count on one hand how many nappies from hell I have dealt with. No mean feat considering the amount of grandchildren I wound up with.

I had no aspirations in judo, other than to get my orange belt, or ever being involved in an Olympics. My special memory of the Olympics was getting up early in the morning as a schoolboy and watching the great Chris Finnegan box his way to a gold medal in 1968. I cannot even say I was that interested when British judo players were fighting at the Olympics in 1980 and 1984 and doing so well. In some ways the tragedy of the terrorist attack in Munich in 1972 was something of a downer that made me realise there is more to life than sport. Anyhow, I duly enrolled at the Polytechnic of Central London in Regent Street where they were running beginners' courses. I had discovered the existence of the club through a magazine called *Floodlight*. This magazine advertised educational courses, academic and sporting, in London. The coach at the Poly was a huge man called William Jones who was a 4th Dan. Even at my age of 26 he was somewhat scary in that he was so powerful looking and as I later learnt very skilful. In an age without the internet it was not possible to track his judo history but the rumour was that he had represented Great Britain and had been one of the nation's top players in his younger days. There was little doubt in my mind after seeing him on the mat that he was an accomplished player and, as I would learn over the next three years, an excellent coach.

I always took pride in myself and had kept myself relatively fit playing table tennis for my office team, the Supreme Court, working at a place called the Court of Protection in Store Street. I was ideally situated for judo training at the Poly just up the road in Regent Street. Sadly I was not prepared for what was to come at a William Jones training session. The warm-up was hard and of the 25 or so students that enrolled the numbers soon dropped off as the weeks passed by. Indeed I too was on the point of quitting until Mr Jones walked past me one evening as I was doing my umpteenth press-up and uttered, 'I'll soon clear off those not serious.' That one sentence saved my judo career (and eventually cost me a fortune) and maybe that of my not-yet-born son Colin from an early extinction and would change the rest of my life. Being a particularly stubborn man there was no way I was going to be driven off this mat regardless of the pain and there was plenty of that. So the scene was set for a 33-year journey that would take me all over the world.

Working in London in the 70s and 80s there were always risks and the security forces were no less vigilant than they are

12

today; there was just more of them. On one trip to the Poly a whole area of Tottenham Court Road was taped off because of a suspect car. Most Londoners had become oblivious to the threats of modern life and saw having to make detours to get from A to B simply as an inconvenience. Not much has changed nowadays. It meant a long detour and a story to tell in the office the following day. I never found out what it was all about.

However, back to the Poly in Regent Street, I was still only keen on winning an orange belt. Not sure why, just simply liked the idea of the colour.

As it happened I did not need to wait too long. A Club Grading was to be held in November 1979 just two months after I walked on to the mat. I had obtained a licence from the British Judo Association (BJA), at that point in my life ignorant to the fact there were other judo associations. It was simply luck that I chose the BJA, something I never regretted.

I arrived one Saturday morning to grade having been made aware by Mr Jones that to move up a belt you had to pass a theory test and then engage in a judo contest against someone of your grade, a novice player roughly the same weight.

In my time in sport I had played many a football match, league table tennis matches and even a school lawn tennis final. I had even played in front of an audience with a couple of pop groups in my early days when I fancied myself as an Eric Clapton, but nothing could have prepared me for a judo contest. The nerves were just unbelievable. Sitting there waiting to be called out for your first opponent was the most nerve-wracking feeling I have ever experienced in my sporting life.

Finally I was called out and, as I faced my first-ever opponent, the nerves vanished, and I set about the task in hand. I knew I had to win one fight to be awarded a yellow belt and I secured a win with a Tai Otoshi (body drop throw). I repeated a similar win in my second contest and was, at the end of the grading, the proud owner of an orange belt, having jumped the yellow at my first attempt. I have to admit my wins were a little sneaky as I had trained with both opponents for some weeks and let them beat me most of the time, all the while saving my body drop speciality until the day of the grading. Both players must have thought it was just a good day but I had actually planned it. I knew by their sizes they would be my likely opponents.

Perhaps I should have quit after a two-month judo career; winning an orange belt hardly suggested I was on course to ever be involved in Olympic judo. As my son Colin would later tell many an interviewer I would probably have been a millionaire had it not been for the countless overseas trips I eventually subsidised.

However, that was never going to be the case. As a proud owner of an orange belt I wanted the next one up; my next target was the green belt. It is strange how quickly you forget the sick nerves before a judo contest, that is until the next time which came about four months later.

This time my task would be much tougher. A couple, maybe three, contests against fellow orange belts. Again that sickening feeling before the contest amazingly cleared as I approached the mat but this time I tasted defeat for the first time to a skilful opponent.

Fortunately I was given one more contest against a much taller player and somehow managed to get underneath his guard and shoulder throw him to be subsequently awarded my lower green belt. This was an interesting contest as I had turned up for the grading having just recovered from a horrible bug and was not feeling very well. During this contest I was being battered and was on the point of quitting until I went underneath him and we both tumbled over. I stood up firmly expecting the referee to award the fight to my opponent but to my surprise it went my way. I had heard rapturous applause as we tumbled and when I gave my name to the control table they both congratulated me on a brilliant throw. As I walked past the referee he whispered, and I quote, 'You don't have a clue, do you?' How right he was; in the days before video I still do not know what went down.

Over the coming months I trained as hard as I could and was even given the privilege by Mr Jones of looking after some of the novices that started after me. One evening he asked me to look after a new French girl. I taught her the usual stuff like breakfalls and O Soto Gari (major outer reap); she had her own judo suit which made life easy. After a hard session a group of us used to go over the road to a pub to rehydrate, usually with lager. After my first encounter with the French girl my friends were raving about how good-looking she was. To their amazement I confessed that I had not noticed; I think it was then I realised that all I ever saw on a judo mat was a person in a judo suit and I have always seen players that way ever since, sometimes not recognising people even today in a supermarket. I have to admit though the following week I did notice what they meant.

The gradings were getting tougher and I thought just maybe I would get to blue belt if I trained hard but beyond that I thought I would struggle somewhat.

It is often said that judo builds confidence and self-belief and nothing could be more true than one night on my journey home from the Poly. I was walking back from Gidea Park station when two gentlemen (loosely put) were sitting outside the shop window of a video shop (remember them?). As I walked past they were clearly poking fun at me and making unsavoury comments. How odd is it that these types all look the same – ugly. What, I wonder, comes first – being an obnoxious human being, or the ugliness? It was the same with the bullies at my school. Anyhow, I had just done a great two-hour session at the Poly and was quite hyped. I actually stopped walking, looked at these would-be male models (if they could have afforded a face job), and contemplated my position. As I learnt through my days in the Crown Court later in life, in a street fight the loser is the victim and the winner is the defendant. In either scenario there was generally a witness statement involved and a sweaty appearance in court to contemplate in one capacity or another. I walked on as anyone with a brain should have done.

As the years rolled into the early 80s, the Thatcher government began cutbacks in subsidies to the local authorities and sports clubs had to increase their fees quadrupling the cost of training at the Poly.

The fact that I was a homeowner with a large mortgage and record-high interest levels (again courtesy of the Thatcher government) forced me to cease attending the club. In fact the Thatcher government had reduced us to buying the cheapest brand products and there was no Aldi to fall back on in the 80s. I was also down to driving a Kermit green 1968 Ford Escort my dad had given me. Yes, I was the original Mr Cool.

At this point I had ground out a lower brown belt. A much higher grade than I ever expected. The gradings at the Poly were for lower-level players and I had now progressed to the higher Kyu Grade which meant I had to travel to the London Judo Society in Balham, London. I had also secured a transfer in my job to the audit section which meant I would be travelling around the country and this would leave little time for judo anyway. So it seemed my interest in judo was at an end. I had reached brown belt, had engaged in about 16 or so judo contests in the process and, courtesy of the London Judo Society gradings, had fought some up-and-coming young players such as Jamie Johnson and James Warren (later to appear in one of my favourite films – *Snatch*) and realised just how high the standard was. I was in little doubt there was no likelihood of further progress. I could now advance to being a middle-aged dad who could take his children to the park on a Sunday morning as I made my way to the mid-life crisis and beer belly that would inevitably be associated with family life.

I made a few appearances at the Romford and Hornchurch Judo Club but in essence I had quit.

Sadly I never did get to thank Mr Jones for his work trying to turn me into a half-decent player and I know not what became of him or the club. Over the years I often wondered if he ever made the connection between Colin and myself?

By this time my daughter Charlotte and my first son David had been born, and over the next four years, my wife Denise and I would be blessed with Colin, in 1983. I am not too sure if 'blessed' is the correct description. Colin was born naturally (probably the last thing natural about him) on 7 June 1983 at Harold Wood Hospital in Essex. I did the hard part of the birth as all men do and was present when he said hello to the world. It was probably the first grey hair he gave me as he did not cry as my first daughter had on delivery. I asked the nurse if this was a problem and got my head bitten off (Jenny Agutter of *Call the Midwife* they were not). He may well have been the easiest of my wife's births but he sure made up for it in the coming years.

Colin showed, from an early age, a very high pain threshold, on one occasion ripping off a flapping fingernail at the age of five. I nearly passed out but Colin did not seem to feel any pain. He started walking so young that he bent his feet inward and would trip over every time he tried to run. The medics told us he would sort the problem out by himself and he did. The determination in this child stood out even as a baby, especially when it was a matter of not doing what he was told. Had I stuck a tennis racket in his hand or enlisted him for rugby or football he would have been a fine player. He was the personification of sport, giving everything from an early age, never giving up.

David, my first son, was a caesarean birth and my first view of him was in an incubator. In truth I walked past him actually expecting a fair child like Charlotte had been and I went to the blond baby who looked really cute. I was redirected to David, who had so much dark hair and to this day he seems able to grow hair at an alarming rate. Our daughter Vicky was born in 1986 to complete the family. Again, another caesarean, and an opportunity to strike back at the nurses and midwives who thought me a hindrance. I was asked by the nurse if I would like to give my daughter a bottle of water. I think she thought she was my first child and much to her amazement I did all the right things in handling and feeding a baby. As she congratulated me I was tempted to punch the air as if I had scored the winner at Wembley but I feared I might drop the baby on her head so decided that was not one of my best ideas.

The mid-80s saw a minor deviation in our martial arts studies as my wife Denise, older daughter Charlotte and David took up karate at the local club in Gidea Park.

Denise rose to brown belt and both Charlotte and David obtained lower grade belts. This style of karate was of the non-striking variety and coming from a hands-on martial art such as judo it was difficult for me to get too enthusiastic about their involvement. There is no doubting it is both skilful and a wonderful confidence boost to those who participate in the sport.

The years passed all too quickly as they do and by 1989 it was clear that David was unhappy at karate and more to the point a five-year-old Colin was beginning to find an interest in sport.

I had moved from my job in audit to a post as court clerk at Snaresbrook Crown Court, a job that gave me a broad insight into criminal law but, more to the point, with our local magistrates' court in Havering being one of our committal courts, I could see first-hand the extent of the drug problem in my local area of Romford. I had previously worked at Inner London Crown Court at the Elephant and Castle and to be fair there was little to choose between the two areas in relation to crime generally. Illicit drugs are a 20th-century curse that will probably be with us for the rest of time but as a father of four I had to consider the best way to protect my children from the dangers. It may seem strange, given many athletes abuse drugs for performance and recreational purposes, nonetheless I took the view if I taught my children to respect their bodies through sport it might just keep them on the straight and narrow. Oddly at this time I did not know of any good children's sessions as I had only attended adult clubs. I did not at this stage figure on judo as a sport for life – this idea was far from my mind.

I was unable to train very often during this period, having effectively quit, but I did manage to get to the Romford and Hornchurch Judo Club one night where I recall having a feisty scrap with a police officer. Well, one thing led to another and we sort of got stuck in as you do resulting in one of the greatest black eyes I ever received. I would add that in this crazy sport we accept we can receive the odd knock and the police officer was a friend who never intended to inflict any injury on me.

Being a court clerk at Snaresbrook I fronted the court sitting just below the judge and that morning I had what was called a section 18 trial which in English translates to a grievous bodily harm with intent. It was a big case with four or five barristers sitting opposite me representing five clearly misunderstood lads. Before the judge came in I could hear the barristers whispering; they seemed to be fascinated by the state of my face. Eventually curiosity got the better of them as one asked, 'What happened to your face?' I assumed it was a reference to my black eye and not just a general observation about my looks and with great delight replied, 'A fight with a copper last night in Romford.' There was a couple of minutes' silence as they pondered my response. No doubt they were wondering which of them would be defending me in the near future, before I gave them the full story. Even the defendants were laughing although their joy only lasted a couple of days. A unanimous conviction and a four-year stretch took the smiles off their faces. My judge was less than impressed that his court clerk looked a bigger thug than the defendants, all of whom had discarded the cloth caps and hoodies for off-the-peg ill-fitting suits to impress the jury (it did not work) but I think he felt safer in my presence than the 300-year-old court usher.

If ever there was a case of fate, David had two friends, John and Robert Evans in and around April 1989 who came over to our house in Hornchurch and both spoke of a judo club at Hornchurch Leisure Centre on a Saturday morning. Neither David nor Colin had any idea their father had ever done judo and Colin had been showing skills with a football at this stage, but it seemed like a good idea and I had little better to do on a Saturday morning, there being no Sky Sports back then, so I thought we would give it a try. I would miss watching *Tiswas* with Chris Tarrant though, and what a show – it was wasted on kids. Okay, so in truth I was really watching the show because of Sally James and what a beauty she was.

The club was called Circles and was run by a coach named Nick Wakefield. I watched as the children trained and there were many on the mat, maybe some 30 children or so. Oddly in the world that we live in today one could be expected to research the coach through the internet to confirm his qualifications and track record but back in 1989 there was no internet and the British Judo Association was almost a one-man band based in London only, it seemed, concerned with the issue of licences. Nothing like the size the Association is today. Also criminal record checks for individuals working with children were many years away. In theory Al Capone could have set up a judo club back then. A very respected coach many years later told me the British Judo Association were great in the 60s and 70s but unfortunately went downhill in the 80s, when they started getting involved in judo (this coach had a hell of a sense of humour). The British Judo Association certainly got their act together over the coming years, in fairness.

In essence it was down to the parent sitting on the sideline to make a judgement, the same as in any sport at that time and what I saw pleased me. Nick Wakefield was a fine coach, very patient and knowledgeable. To this day I do not know if the club was affiliated to the British Judo Association or whether Mr Wakefield was a British Judo Association coach. All I knew was that my sons had a great Saturday morning and Mr Wakefield did a great job.

Most of the children were under eight and in those days not eligible for a BJA licence in any event, so Mr Wakefield used to run gradings for under-eights along the same lines as a BJA one but instead of awarding belt colours would award 'circles' for their belts.

My sons had been attending the club for a few months and as I got to know Mr Wakefield better it became apparent to him that I had a history in judo and, as I found out many years later, no self-respecting judo coach will leave alone a parent that once did the sport and so Nick asked me to come on the mat and gently get back into it.

My return to the mat started with a groundwork tussle with Nick. What an eye-opener that turned out to be. After just a few minutes on the ground with Nick I was blacking out. It was not that Nick was much bigger than I was but he was certainly stronger, fitter and much more skilful than me and that combination spelt rest or blackout. It could not be said that I was unfit per se but clearly being fit is not the same as being fit for judo.

Anyhow, it seemed like a good idea to get back on the mat so I started to train after the boys on a Saturday morning. What a sacrifice giving up *Tiswas* and Sally James for judo. More to the point Nick had planned a grading so it would be my first opportunity to see my boys fight for the first time.

Sadly, this was just before the video age. However, I remember David won two and lost two and fought very well. Colin on the other hand lost both his opening fights to children much bigger but never stopped trying. Nick decided to match him with a little girl who had also lost both contests. Back then it was not uncommon to match boys against girls at five or six years old.

My son managed by the skin of his teeth to just edge out the little girl, who was no easy opponent, for what was his first-ever judo victory. Neither the little girl nor her parents will ever likely know she lost to an eventual double Olympian and double European medallist as well as a Commonwealth champion.

Quite frankly, if at that grading the ghost of futures to come arrived and told me then what lay ahead, I would have died laughing. However, what a shame there were not the betting opportunities of today – what odds would I have got for this five-year-old boy being an Olympian?

In the months that passed, Colin persevered and started to look okay on the mat, and by the time we reached the point of the next grading I had higher expectations of him.

The grading was held at a hall in Dagenham and this time Colin took apart two opponents with clinical ease given he was still only five years old but what followed was beyond my imagination. At these gradings Nick would quite rightly try to give everyone a win and so when Colin was matched up to be a boy's 'sacrificial' goat, I had no problem with that. I supported his view of encouraging children in this manner. However, Colin again destroyed his bigger opponent to secure win number three. Nick then gave him an even bigger boy and again Colin threw him within seconds. At this point I had lost touch of the fact that older brother David had turned in another solid performance, winning two contests. It became clear to me Colin was showing real potential.

We had struck up six wins on the day and, as I was leaving the hall, a coach of another judo club, Terry Adams, took me to one side and advised me to step up my sons to a bigger club. Advice I decided to take on board.

In the late 80s and early 90s judo was very much more popular in Great Britain than it is today. The past 20 years or so has shown a growth in different strains of martial arts which has split the audience so to speak but so popular was judo that Hornchurch Leisure Centre housed not just Nick Wakefield's Circles judo club but a huge club called the Kyu Shin Kwai coached by Doug Wilson.

I watched the club a few times and decided that a move here would be progress so we ceased going to Circles and joined the Kyu Shin Kwai. It was due to Doug that I set out on the pathway toward being a coach. Doug often let me take the warm-up on a Monday evening and I really enjoyed helping out with the novices.

At this time I was battling again at the London Judo Society judo gradings in Balham in a bid to win my black belt. Time and time again I ventured to London and always I came back pointless as well as sore. To win a black belt in judo back then you had to win two preliminary contests during the morning and then win a line-up beating three brown belts in succession without a break or beat brown belts on a 7-point score or a 10-point score and accrue 100-points over a period of time; this is still the way it's done competitively but you now have the option to go down the theoretical route. Being a 36-year-old man I was classified as a veteran player so had the concession of only needing 75-points rather than 100 for a younger man.

As far as I was concerned the number of points could have been 20; I was not good enough to win a contest. In fairness

I was working five days a week and many of the players who beat me every month were Great Britain squad players, some of whom were full-time players at the Neil Adams Centre in Coventry training five days a week. In fact the list of players that beat me reads like a who's who of judo of that period.

My monthly visits were made pleasant by a very nice lady that constantly asked me if I was over 30 when I registered. I was flattered until one day some guy in front of me, who looked like a zombie long before they were fashionable, was asked the same question; she was clearly being polite rather than the question reflecting the age I looked.

However, I always seemed to draw these young players. That was until I met a canny lad from the Tyne who gave me some tips. You might think it was advice on my style or my tactics. No, it was where to stand in the queue. He told me that whenever someone walked into the London Judo Society hall, all the young guys would take a look and, if it was an older player, try and stand behind them on the basis the names would be close on the sheet and they would match you accordingly, as long as there was not too much disparity in size. Clearly an older man was a prime target for a fit young athlete and looking back what he was telling me was that the players were eyeing me up as an easy 10-point win.

So I watched next time and he was right. I even saw some cheeky swine move from the front of the queue to behind me. That was it, I went to the toilet and watched who was coming in and, yes, the plan was to stand behind an older guy if I could find one – it was not that easy. Wait I did, and what luck, in walked the oldest-looking judoka I had ever seen, so I made a dash to stand behind him and, what do you know, we were matched. What could go wrong? Sadly I had something of a conscience and decided to let the fight run a minute or two before moving in mercilessly for the kill. I wanted to give him his money's worth. The old sod caught me for a seven score and that was that. I battered him for the next 30 seconds or so but to no avail. I got him next month, though I moved like an eagle and took him out. Yes, I stood behind him again in the queue, well fair's fair?

Seriously, one should never underestimate any player in sport. The next month I had managed to sandwich between two older players and I started to accumulate the points. Now, don't get me wrong, this did not mean I was knocking over all the over 30s because I was not. Some of those older guys were good fighters and I took my share of defeats.

Through the help of Doug and the Kyu Shin Kwai club I managed to grind out a couple of wins over players my age or thereabouts from this point onwards.

Meanwhile, Colin and David were preparing for their first-ever judo competition at Abbs Cross School in Hornchurch, organised by the Kyu Shin Kwai. The club at that time had an enormous membership of around 300 players and the club tournament always attracted around 120 of them. Despite my experience of judo grading contests I had never attended a tournament before so this was a learning exercise for the family.

First up was David who won a contest but lost his next two and went out. Colin, in the under-eight-years-old section, won five contests in a row to secure a gold medal.

He had continued in the same vein as the last grading he fought at the Circles Club. He actually asked his mum if his dad was proud of him.

It was the first-ever judo medal won by a family member and took pride of place on the mantelpiece; many years later most of these medals would find their way into black dustbin bags but at that time we were very proud parents. Colin Oates's long journey that would take him all over the world had begun at a school in Hornchurch, Essex; indeed, one I may well have attended had I not failed the eleven-plus.

Just when life seemed to be settled I was offered a job in Norwich, which meant we would have to move home and not just leave our family and friends but lose the social side of my boys enjoying their time at a great judo club, and my wife and daughter Charlotte would lose their karate club too.

The move was too good to refuse and in April 1991 we moved from our home of ten years in Hornchurch to the tiny village of North Lopham in Norfolk. Driving past the Village Hall, where our club would eventually operate from, in our 1977 Ford Cortina estate en route to our new house, I never imagined even then what the future would hold. We had a dog called Ben at the time and we had given him a tranquilliser for the journey. Of course it did not work until we got to the house and then, and only then, he passed out. The dog was an amazing character, being the only member of the family to spend a night in Diss police station (to my knowledge anyhow) after going out for a solo walk one evening and getting apprehended. They probably took him into custody for stalking some bitch in the next village;

it was never made clear what his offence was but the mangy mutt cost me £70 to get back.

I also remember walking into the Kings Head pub in North Lopham for the first time. As Denise and I entered the bar it seemed all the conversation ceased. It went totally silent. I expected that at any moment someone would approach us and say they did not like strangers in this town and show me their gun. Little did we know then but the successive owners of that pub and the people of North Lopham would in just a few years' time raise huge amounts of money to support not just Colin Oates but their local judo club and we would succeed in putting Lopham on the television and radio.

Saying goodbye to the Kyu Shin Kwai was hard. I had so much respect for Doug Wilson. At times I thought he was a little cynical about the sport but when I look back on his history it is easy to see why. Doug was behind and had produced a number of eventual Olympians but those players had either left his club prior to their rise to Olympic fame or had been poached by other clubs, mostly the latter, and there never seemed to be any mention of the base he had built for those athletes. There was no doubt in my mind that Doug was the inspiration of many of those players. Later in my life I too would suffer those same experiences and feelings of losing players at the Olympic stage so would eventually fully appreciate how coaches become cynical. Although my two players were never actually poached in that way I did in many ways feel I had lost them. Doug was never attributed the credit for his input into a number of fine players, but that is judo.

Despite moving up to Norfolk I kept in touch with the Kyu Shin Kwai and often travelled by train there, but the cost proved too great and our final appearance with the club would be a tournament to be held in the summer of 1991.

Before moving to North Lopham I had checked with the BJA as to the nearest club, which was the Diss Judo Club run by Chris Clancy.

On a Thursday evening we packed our bags and strolled down the A1066 to join the club.

The club in Diss was a small one with maybe about 18 children and seven or eight adults. Although they did not consider themselves a competition club in the true sense, they did a team fight at the end of the session which kept the competitive edge of my sons on the sharp side. Sadly my wife and daughter Charlotte were unable to find a local karate club that recognised their belt ranks and so they gave up karate and both started to train in judo at Diss.

The coach, Chris Clancy, was not happy to let my youngest daughter Vicky on the mat as she was just five years old at the time so it meant we now had five family members doing judo with Vicky having to wait her turn.

It became clear to me that the boys would need two nights a week of training and I found that at the other end of the A1066 there was a club in Thetford, run by Stewart Collings (who would become a pillar of support as time went on) and this too was a well-run club with around 20 or so children. The senior class, however, consisted of 20 to 30 seniors, run by a Great Britain International, Paul Adams. I was aware of the existence of this club as I had graded at an Eastern Area Grading in January 1991 before we had moved.

The session Paul ran was brilliant. I was a very poor brown belt and through Paul I felt my game continue to improve, so much so that I started to consider perhaps entering the National Veterans tournament at High Wycombe. Every Wednesday was a painful experience, the evening was in essence one big punch-up, but it was an addiction. It was a session you always gave second thoughts to attending because of the intensity, but after, when you were returning home from it, you had a kind of buzz. They were truly memorable evenings.

The summer Kyu Shin Kwai tournament was looming and Colin was about to defend his gold medal. It was July 1991 and we journeyed back to Hornchurch and the Abbs Cross School one last time fully expecting another gold medal. The good news was Turan Kiani, a real seven-year-old prospect and our main rival, was in a different weight group so the way was clear. Unfortunately sport does not work that way and Colin got beaten in the final by a young lad named Chris James and had to be content with a silver medal.

This was the beginning of the video age and I hired a camera (they were too expensive to buy at that time) and recorded all of Colin and David's fights. They are the earliest recordings of both boys fighting. I would add that the camera was both huge and awkward. It had to be carried in a massive case. Technology advanced in leaps and bounds in the coming years to a point where the mobile phone in your pocket could produce better quality video.

We lost touch with Doug in the years that followed but the Kyu Shin Kwai carried on even though many of their competition players either left the club or were poached. I do not know for sure but I think the club no longer exists but I did hear of the sad passing of Doug Wilson, a man we owed so much to.

The next event a member of the family would fight in would be the British Veterans tournament in High Wycombe. I would be the first in the family to engage in a national-level tournament – it would be the first of many National Championships the family would fight in – and I had no expectations whatsoever. With just 20-points toward my black belt, all I wanted was the opportunity to fight players my age and weight (often at gradings I could give many kilos away as well as youth).

My wife and I booked a hotel in High Wycombe on the Friday night as I could weigh in the evening. Fighting at -60k it was always something of a struggle to make weight but in weighing the night before it is possible to see the amount of players in your group, in my case seven fighters. In retrospect it was probably a bad idea. At 38 years old I was about to fight a tournament, a National Championship at that. Having effectively starved myself all week (well, cut out the apple pies), I returned to the hotel feeling so sick I could not eat. Also staying at the hotel were a team from Newcastle and, try as they might, even with their wacky sense of humour, they could not make me feel any better.

The night before a competition a judo player will probably fight 200 contests in their mind and I was no exception. Given most of the time you will be lucky to fight even two the following day, it is somewhat a waste of energy, even if it is only in your head. I drove to High Wycombe with rock music blasting out of my car cassette in a bid to lift my game. Young guys would be listening to rap music but my music would be John Mellencamp, true quality rock. I had failed to eat breakfast so tanked up on chocolate and bananas.

The wonderful thing about being the lowest weight is the fact you are the first group called so there is not too much waiting to fight. My first contest was against the defending champion Malcolm Ellis and, as I walked out to face him, amazingly, just like at the gradings, the nerves vanished. I won the fight with two 7-point scores. Being in a pool of four meant I simply needed to win one more and I was likely to be in the semi-final and, more to the point, the win over Malcolm Ellis was 10 more points toward my black belt, the main purpose of entering the event. My next fight, however, was a nightmare; leading by a 7, I found myself thrown for a winning 10-point throw, which now meant I had to win my next fight or I was eliminated. I set out in my third fight to take no chances and beat my opponent with a hold down. As I saw the clock ticking down I knew it had taken me into the semi-final and at the very least a bronze medal.

The semi-final was later in the day and I walked out much more relaxed as the job had been done, but it was not to end there. I threw my opponent for a 10-point win, only to hear a Geordie accent, I think the voice of Jon Pounder, yelling, 'You can eat your breakfast now.' I had reached a National final at my first attempt.

The final was an anti-climax as I tussled over with my opponent and was adjudged to have been thrown. When I shook hands with the other fighter he said he had no idea what that was all about, and that just about summed up the situation.

Perhaps that was my first brush with a referee's decision I failed to understand. In truth the player that beat me would have thrown me at some point in the contest. All day I thought he was good but I would have preferred to have really lost. Even looking at a video replay, I failed to comprehend the decision, especially coming from a top referee at that time. We simply tumbled over, there was no throw involved, but that was judo and there was no sense in dwelling on decisions.

We returned to Norfolk in pounding rain but on a high note, 30 black belt points and a silver National medal was my proud achievement, but my judo was secondary to that of my sons and anything I was doing was for their long-term benefit, and our attention must next focus on Colin's first official BJA competition, the Haverhill Mini Mons in October 1991.

It was in truth the first real children's competition I had attended, as the Kyu Shin Kwai events were friendly. We, the parents, all knew each other and somehow those two events had been somewhat civilised. I was soon to find out the realities of junior judo.

Without really knowing how good Colin was, we did not know what to expect. I think deep down I thought Colin would knock over these kids just like in London. There were two groups of four with a cross-over semi-final so it did not seem too difficult; two wins and usually your player is in the semi-final. All went according to plan in Colin's first fight – a comfortable win – but the second fight was quite different. Colin's opponent Kevin Addison from the Kumuichi Judo Club in King's Lynn made Colin look weak and he easily beat him. When this happens, as a dad, you look for excuses. I remember thinking the other lad was bigger, older and more experienced. You feel they are under-graded or the referee was harsher on your son than the opponent. It only occurs to you many years later the boy your son was fighting was simply better but that is so hard to admit.

Colin managed to reach the semi-final where another boy, Craig Peters from Feltwell Judo Club, beat him and so we had to settle for a bronze. Again you look for the same excuses. The lesson I did learn was that clubs that turned up en masse seemed to have a parent base that could make it very difficult for the player without that same backing. The heavy cheering for your son or daughter's opponent can, at first, upset you as a parent and even at times angers you but regardless of your feelings it was and still is part of the junior circuit. Both Kevin Addison and Craig Peters would figure in some way in Colin's development over the next few years as rivals at local level.

Toward the end of 1991 I completed a coaching course. I do not recall if I had aspirations of running my own club at that time but I did want to learn how to improve my family.

By 1992 all the Oates family were training somewhere, as I had found a club in Brandon run by Maurice Thorpe, another excellent coach and true gentleman, that took five- and six-year olds, which meant my youngest daughter, not able to train at Thetford or Diss, could now be part of the team, so to speak.

Throughout the year we participated in competitions up and down the country with a high level of success. My two daughters were winning medals as well as Colin but older brother David was struggling at this time.

It was in 1992 that I first experienced the spectator fee – an event in Wanstead, Essex – and to this day I fail to understand it. Without the parent at a children's event there is no competitor, so how can you implement that charge? Years later it would shape how Denise would run tournaments in the East of England and even today we will never charge spectators, as to our minds it is a dishonest fee. It could be loaded on to the competition fee maybe.

The expense of travelling to different judo clubs as well as the cost of the competitions was having a profound effect on my finances. Something had to give as my car was covering thousands of miles per month with the knock-on effect of wear and tear but the bug had caught hold of all of us. If there was a tournament we had to be there; it mattered not if we could afford it.

A tournament that needs special mention is the Willesden International. This was a truly magnificent event attracting many overseas judo clubs. In May 1992 the entry in David's weight category totalled 63 players and in Colin's category there were 37 players. In David's case it is true to say it matters not how many players are in your group– it only takes one or two (depending on the competition system) to knock you out and that was exactly what happened.

However, Colin battled to the semi-final and a fight with a Dutch boy. I was, to say the least, a little alarmed that there was a Dutch referee and Dutch line judge, the other judge being British. The fight was tough and back then if there was no score the officials would give a decision by holding up flags at the end of the contest. To my horror the fight went to a decision and I kind of knew which way it was going when the Dutch female referee patted the Dutch boy on the head as she went to collect her flags. Well of course it was a 2-1 split to the Dutch boy. This decision brought my usual protests. What was unusual and not expected at judo tournaments was the emergence of a 'flying' Dutchman wielding a knife in my direction and threatening to slice me. Fortunately, he gave more thought to his predicament and took off somewhere. I often wondered what became of this cheerful chap. He was probably the first real idiot I encountered at an event, but sadly by no means would he be the last.

Anyway, back to the judo and Colin was left with a bronze medal final that he won. We returned home with a magnificent trophy as was the norm for this tournament. On trying to return to our car for our trip home we had to take a detour because the police had cordoned off the road that led directly to where we were parked. Apparently there had been a violent crime committed down this particular street. It really was that kind of weekend.

The tale does not even end there as Steven Flanagan, who was another of my players, battled to a final that day and collected a brilliant silver medal for himself and the club. We returned home very contented (once we got to our car) but, three days later at Thetford Judo Club, Stewart Collings asked if I heard what happened to Steven at the weekend? My reply was simple enough, being, and I quote, 'Yes, fantastic wasn't it?' Stewart looked somewhat amazed and responded by telling me Steven had been hit by a Transit van whilst out on his bike on the Sunday. Needless to say I explained I was talking about his medal the day before. Fortunately Steven made a complete recovery and went on to take a medal at the prestigious Liberty Bell tournament in the USA some years later. Today he is a successful photographer.

We realised that we had to find a club that catered just for competition judo and the club Craig Peters attended at Feltwell fitted the requirement. At this club Vicky too was welcome and suddenly we had the backing of a rowdy bunch of parents that were capable of intimidating my family's opponents at competitions. The club was run by Richard Ashton, who I had actually met when I fought him at the London Judo Society grading some years earlier. He was an excellent trainer and a first-class referee.

By mid-1992 Colin's reputation as a cadet player was beginning to take off, as was evidenced by the rampant cheer that went up from the Jodan Judo Club after Robert Wyles beat my son in the final of an event in Sheerness called the Island judo competition. Their coach apologised for the outburst, which I took as flattery. I was in no way offended by their response. This would also turn out to be the last year I would wear a wedding ring after being slung out at the National Veterans Championship in Gateshead. It was the opening fight of the day and I think I was still asleep. A simple error in not removing a ring proved costly. For such a long journey it was a harsh way to lose a contest I was otherwise winning, my opponent pointing to the ring after I had notched up the lead in the contest. My only other fight was a mauling from Colin Small.

It was also the year I fought in younger men tournaments. I had travelled to Milton Keynes for the Renzoko tournament and had entered myself as well as Colin. It was one of those days where you get out of bed and just do not feel like it. So when I got there I told the nice tournament organiser, a man named Ray Taylor, I had forgotten my licence. He then told me he knew I was up to date and that was no problem. I then said I had forgotten my suit; no problem again, he had a spare. I then confessed I had brought the suit but was not really in the mood. Again, no problem, there were only three of us in the group and I would be doing him a favour. I thought, just two contests, I can handle that. Not so, there were five of us which meant four fights.

My first contest against an 18-year-old gorilla nearly killed me. I scored an early 7-pointer and spent five minutes defending it. At the end of the fight I collapsed in a heap by the edge of the mat. The table tried to call me on two fights later but took one look at me and gave me another five minutes to recover. I won two and lost two that day and got a bronze. I was only able to walk in a straight line about four days later. Looking back I am pleased I fought as it was one of my better performances but it really hurt. In fact, just writing this, it still hurts. Of course, Colin made winning a gold medal that day look easy with five straight wins, as was often the case.

Our time at Diss Judo Club was coming to an end – many years later we would eventually return and save the club from extinction – but for now and throughout 1992 and 1993 competition experience for Colin, David and Charlotte was the order of the day with Colin clearly beginning to stand out as a quality player. I could, however, be very grateful to Chris Clancy and Diss Judo Club as he showed me a gentler approach to coaching non-competitive children which would be very valuable to me some years later but, even more importantly, he showed me the power of the press. Any accomplishment a Diss player achieved, Chris would send a report to the *Diss Express*, and parents, myself included, loved seeing their children's names in the local paper.

Indeed I remembered how proud I was back in 1967 when the *Romford and Hornchurch Recorder* reported the goal (yes, it was the goal and one of not many) I scored for Rainham Rangers. I still have the cutting to this day. Reporting judo results to the local press was not something I would ever have thought of but, even after we moved from Diss to the Feltwell club, I continued to report the family results to the *Diss Express* who would strike up a very close relationship with the Oates judo family and Kumo Judo Club over the next 20 years.

Training and fighting out of the Feltwell club was not without problems. The club was full of highly skilled players and without doubt the most prolific medal-winning club in the Eastern Area (which consisted of Norfolk, Suffolk and Cambridgeshire) at that time and the coach Richard Ashton was a great coach. However, with competitive junior players there are more competitive parents, and relationships between each became strained as time went on. We felt a little like gatecrashers at a wedding, not truly accepted, especially being from London.

As a family, we had the key tournament of the year in our sights, the Junior Nationals held at Crystal Palace in November. At this time, if your child reached a National final, they would gain entry to the British Cadet squad and on selection for any overseas trip would be given their Union Jack flag to sew on to the judo suit jacket. The flag was to many a parent and child alike more important than the medal. In fact it made your child stand out at judo competitions, as often you would target beating the player with the flag and the winning of a medal was less important.

In 1993 Colin was still too young to compete at the Junior Nationals but David and Charlotte were eligible. The selection process in the East was by managers appointed by the Area Committee who took into account their competition record and their attendance at organised squad sessions held at Breckland Leisure Centre. There was an Eastern Area competition that was closed to players that were members of clubs within the East only, and as such it was also possible to identify the Area champions. It seemed a simple process to me but the catch was that only two players per weight and age group could be selected, which meant if there were three excellent players aged 12 and in the -31k weight group the Area manager could only select two which meant, unless one wanted to fight up a weight (not ideal), they could not attend the premier event of the year.

The Eastern Area was then and still is one of the smaller of the British Judo Association's 12 regions consisting of, in 1993, about 40 clubs, and given that many clubs are non-competitive, fighting junior players were not that much in abundance and as such the squad was not huge. It is not being too unkind to suggest that as a small area with a limited amount of volunteers running the committee, squads and area competitions, the individuals involved were very close-knit, to say the least. We, as ex-Londoners, were very much the outsiders. I was told, when we moved in to the village of North Lopham, it would take some 25 years to be accepted as a local. So I always knew that we were on the outside looking in. I was aware that David was unlikely to be selected as there were two players in his age and weight that were clearly more successful than him so he was out of the picture. On the other hand Charlotte had a good year and met the eligibility of area squad selection in that she had attended the squad sessions and had won many medals that year. The *Diss Express* had a picture on their back page of Charlotte with her medal haul for the year and a headline, 'Charlotte waits with bated breath.' It seemed all we needed to do was wait for the letter of selection with details of the weekend. Every morning we waited and every evening I told my 14-year-old daughter, on her return home from school, we will get the letter tomorrow.

The letter never arrived. I complained to a member of the Eastern Area Committee who explained they (the squad managers) did not consider her good enough to go. There seemed to be no appeal process and no transparency as to the whole selection, with players with less medals than Charlotte selected, even some Charlotte had beaten that year. As a parent I was outraged; I expected the Feltwell Judo Club to take up her case, but soon realised that nobody there cared either. The parents, the coach were preoccupied with their own children as you would expect. We were on our own. The girl selected in place of Charlotte did not medal; looking back this is not to say that Charlotte would have taken a medal either. It was the lack of clarity in the selection process that troubled me.

That year the family haul of National medals increased with a further Veterans silver medal I won at High Wycombe, but it was of little consolation as all my efforts in judo were geared to promote and improve the family, especially Colin. I was learning more lessons, however, and discovering that players seemed to have a better chance of squad selection if they attended sessions at the Area squad manager's club or the managers were your mates. I had also discovered that other areas as small as the East ran selection trials for the Nationals which made me wonder why there was ever a need for a subjective selection process which often demoralised other children and their parents, not just my daughter who truly felt she had qualified her selection with her results. This was never likely to be an option I would choose.

I had recently passed my coaching course and was able to start my own club if I felt the need. The experiences of Charlotte had left me with a bitter taste with the Eastern Area selection process and the Feltwell Judo Club where we were never truly comfortable.

At this stage I believed that a trials system was preferable rather than a process based on subjective selection. Ironically this view would change in 2005 when Colin and I were presented with the trials from hell.

I had struck up a friendship with the coaches of Kevin Addison, who Colin had lost to in his first BJA competition and who ran Kumuichi Judo Club in King's Lynn, and it was through Chris Payne and Jo Brook we would taste our first experience of overseas judo which would in turn shape Colin's style and development over the coming years. At this stage I realised that Colin was a cut above the rest and I saw with overseas connections there would be advantages to him experiencing continental judo at an early stage in his career.

THE DEVELOPMENT YEARS
1994–2000

AN OVERSEAS trip to Bavay, France was being organised by Kumuichi Judo Club, and Chris Payne their senior coach had kindly invited us to make up the numbers and combine with his club. So this became our priority. The whole family could go to Bavay. My wife Denise had by now given up going on the mat but the rest of us could train and fight in France. This seemed to be progression whilst we considered our future club options in Norfolk. I was unaware just how good French judo was or how popular it was in Europe at that time. We were not affluent money-wise back then and it seemed a great way to take the family abroad at a very low price. We would be housed with French families, leaving only the cost of travel. The weekend was fantastic. The nonsense one hears that the French hate the British? Totally untrue; we were treated like royalty, even given champagne after a hard training session. The competition was well run and we had mixed success as a family, returning home with an insight into international judo.

The overseas trip, however enjoyable, was a distraction from the bigger issues of where we should be training. I had the qualifications to start a club but not the money to buy the mats. In 1994 there was no eBay where you could buy cheap mats or UKSport offering start-up grants; trying to find second-hand mats was very problematic.

We started to sell all sorts of items at Banham boot sale, clearing many a classic vinyl album. We hated every minute. Nonetheless, we made money, well enough to buy one mat. As far as we were concerned it was a start. We have in recent years lent mats to many a club that was starting up as we appreciated back then and do now how difficult it is. Fortunately nowadays there are many grant applications which makes it a little easier to create a sports club.

My family have always been close and that included my mother and my brother and, when I let slip in conversation that we had raised some £120 or so at a boot sale, my mother hated the idea that we were having to do this and insisted on sending me a cheque for £1,000. It was another example of my mother always seemingly knowing when I needed help. It was not the first time she had helped me out; it was not the last either. My mother never liked the sport and even when I hit my fifties she constantly told me to quit both fighting and the coaching. Sadly she did not live long enough to see our proudest moments in the sport, leaving us a couple of years before the London Olympics.

With my mother's financial input we were now in a strong position to start a club and become independent. The next stage would be to find a hall. My first choice would be Lopham Village Hall but on inspection the floor area was reduced by the existence of a stage that would be a serious hazard to judo players. Next in line was the Garboldisham Village Hall. I was told of the hall by the guide leader there whose son had been a judo player at Diss. It was ideal and the Monday night was available. There was a slightly cynical reason why we were allowed into the hall. The hall had been very much monopolised by a bowls club and I believe they and the Garboldisham Village Hall committee had been in the process of obtaining grants to update the hall. It was a time when various charities started throwing money at rural areas to improve facilities. The committee was being stifled by the fact that the hall had to prove a cross-section of the society used the hall in order to obtain grant aid and, as children are not known to be keen on bowls and the guide movement did not yield huge numbers, the introduction of a judo club for children ticked another box on the grant application.

At the time, it was the best offer, but they refused to give me storage space for the mats I had bought so I had to buy an old Bedford CF250 to store the mats we had purchased in the garage.

It was less than ideal, especially if it was raining or cold, but it was local and we had no other options. The transportation of mats from one site to another is a recipe for disaster, especially in the days of the 2x1 metre mats which were heavy and awkward to move. Eventually, when the van broke down, the hall amazingly, rather than lose our letters needed for their grant applications, found us some storage space.

It was not the first time the van had let us down either. On our way to a club we ran in Botesdale I decided to see if the van could hover at 50 miles per hour through a huge flood in a remote country lane. Unfortnately, Bedford CF250s seem incapable of flying over water and it meant a nightmare two-mile walk in darkness to the village telephone box in Redgrave, in the days before the mobile phone. This left me having to ring the RAC and explain where we were. Questions like what am I opposite, any landmarks? How do you explain to someone clearly from a town there is a field on the left, the right, in front and behind, and my van is knee deep in water in a pitch-black country lane with no street lights? It took two hours for the rescue to arrive and to add insult to injury we received a barrage of complaints on the phone the following day from parents whose kid's night was ruined by us not running a class.

When I parted with my first car, a 1961 Ford Anglia 105E, I was quite upset; when we got rid of the van we broke out the champagne. Well, okay, so it was Cava, but we still celebrated.

Anyhow, by now I had become highly cautious of the people I was dealing with, both in judo and beyond, and I had my doubts about how long we might be at Garboldisham – I was aware they needed letters from me to obtain a grant for a new hall – so in naming the club, it had to be a mobile name, one not linked to any village.

The Lopham fen is famous for being the home of Britain's largest spider, the raft spider. I personally hate the things but it seemed a link to a local name. I researched the word for spider in Japanese and I think (I have never been sure) it is Kumo but spelt 'Kumho' in western-style letters. It mattered not in the end as it was a name that was transportable which meant I could take it anywhere.

In May 1994 Kumo Judo Club was formed. Few of my contemporaries would have noticed in the Eastern Area at that time, but the club would not just change the area, in time it would very much control it, and along the way produce a host of quality players.

The Stowmarket under-18 would be the first outing for a club that consisted of five members of the Oates family and maybe six other child members. The first-ever Kumo medal was actually won by a little girl named Jessie Kristofferson – a bronze medal that her father told me hung over her bed from that day onward. Jessie later returned to Denmark with her parents and today she is a veterinary surgeon in Ireland.

We were now entering the serious stuff of developing Colin, who had some serious rivals in the area and, given the unclear selection process on area representation at the Junior Nationals we had already experienced with Charlotte, we had to make sure Colin's selection would be almost automatic. We had mixed results against Craig Peters and we were always rivals (not enemies) even when fighting for the same Feltwell club so I did not want to let Craig forge ahead on wins. So at Stowmarket I took the decision to move Colin up a weight group to avoid another confrontation with his rival. There was little prospect of a medal at the higher weight so it seemed a good idea. However, Colin progressed to the final of the under 38ks, throwing all in his path and, although he lost the final, he was awarded the Ippon Trophy for the most 10-point throws on the day.

As a new club we were delighted with the award and it seemed, finally, Colin was being recognised as a real prospect. Sadly things are not always what they seem and a complaint was made that the trophy should have been awarded to another player. The suggestion was that Colin, a ten-year-old boy, should be stripped of the trophy some days after the award. It was obvious that Colin had been recognised within our area but not for the right reasons; it had become clear to me he was seen as a threat to the players who considered themselves elite.

The attitudes of some people I was now encountering was beginning to seriously trouble me. We were doing a sport that had little profile as far as the media were concerned yet we seemed to be attracting more and more hostility within our local area, some of which appeared to be just plain nastiness.

Eventually the dispute was resolved and the original decision was in fact correct and we kept the trophy. Looking back, should we ever have cared? At the time we did because most parents then and now still believe what you do as a junior/cadet actually matters. Not one player at that competition other than Colin made any high-level international impact to my knowledge and recollection so with the benefit of hindsight it might have been better if another player had been awarded the trophy.

During this time I received an unexpected boost, a telephone call from Riddlesworth Hall, a private prep school (where Lady Diana had attended many years earlier) requesting a meeting with me. The proposal was to set up a judo club within the school. Driving into the school grounds for the first time was an awe-inspiring feeling, an indication of not just how the other half live, more like perhaps how the chosen minority gain such an advantage in later life. The school was set in beautiful surroundings with their own swimming pool and chapel and acres of playing fields, a world apart from normal life.

My meeting with the headmistress, whose name I have now forgotten, was a success, even if it was conducted whilst on a walk of the grounds during which her dog decided to take the biggest dump I have ever seen descend from the backside of any animal. So difficult to remain focused on a conversation in such circumstances with one eye on a dog. The mat fees would be very much higher than I would normally receive. It really was an offer I could not refuse. The only stumbling block was that I wanted to bring Colin to the classes. My main concern was to safeguard myself as this was an all girls' school and I was to be otherwise alone in a gym with a dozen or so 12-year-old girls. After some bartering I got her to agree to them letting my 15-year-old daughter Charlotte assist on the sessions.

They did not have any gym mats worthy of judo, so every Thursday evening I would have to drive this old Bedford CF250 to the school, often driving past Bentleys and cars the like of which I had only previously seen in the cinema; it was often embarrassing – my truck was that tatty it would have aroused the interest of the flying squad if I had ever driven the thing in London.

They were brilliant kids in every respect but without realising it they could make you feel very inadequate with comments like

'I sank daddy's boat last week'. I imagined it was some 12-foot dinghy until she told me she had left the porthole open. I asked how big this boat was and received the reply that it was 22-foot long and it was the smallest of the three they owned but they had now refloated the sunken one. She really was not boasting, it was just a natural conversation.

During the two years we operated out of Riddlesworth Hall we generated sufficient mat fees to travel the country as a club and we ended our operations there after two years with the demise of the van. There is one prank the girls tried to pull off worthy of mention. One evening I had packed the mats away and on this occasion my younger daughter Vicky was with me. We both got into the van and something did not seem right but I started the engine, reversed the van ready to exit the school and, for some reason, I decided to check the back doors of the van. On opening the door I found one of the girls hiding behind the mats with a grin on her face. To this day I am not sure how I could have explained this to the school or the law had I driven off.

There was never a chance of finding an Olympic prospect in that bunch of crazy kids but they were a pleasure to teach, not without skill, as some of them were talented, but their futures were for a different world. I often wonder if any of them are running the country now or remember us at all.

There was one other short-lived judo club I ran to make money for our travels worthy of mention. This was a state comprehensive at Hartismere in Eye, Suffolk. In Norfolk/Suffolk the martial arts lines are drawn; there are some towns dominated by karate, others by tae kwon do, while some are controlled by judo. Crossing those lines is near-on impossible as there are high demands on low numbers of willing participants. The town of Eye is a kickboxing/tae kwon do town and judo was never likely to succeed. However, I can claim to have made the most incorrect comment in the history of judo. A girl who had been training with me at Lopham walked past me in the gym while I was standing with three teachers at the school and she brightly said hello to me. Never having seen her in anything but a judo suit I simply replied, 'Hello Laura, you look so different with clothes on.' I did try to explain to the teachers what I meant, but like I have already said I only see a judo suit on my mat.

The club continued to grow and Denise, who had quit going on the mat, turned her focus to judo administration and assisted in the running of judo competitions in the East. As the year progressed we turned our attentions to the Junior Nationals. We had already been hit once by what we considered a flawed selection system but we followed the criteria, loose as it was, and I had now also become an area referee. This happened because, as a young coach with a fast-growing paranoia complex in the sport, I had become something of a matside animal, moaning and groaning at referees, getting involved in rows with parents and coaches alike at competitions in and out of the Eastern Area. A senior referee named Derek Coult eventually approached me and told me if I could do a better job then I should do it. I took up the challenge and became an area referee.

It did the trick to a degree. I no longer complained at genuine errors as I saw how difficult the task was. To this day I still doubt the objectivity, even honesty, of some referees at times but that is a different issue altogether and not just restricted to the British judo scene but other sports too. I spoke to a gymnastics coach who told me the perils of simply crossing the border from England into Wales and vice versa with referees whose objectivity is often in doubt. Modern technology has improved the situation and it is much rarer to find decisions that are as harsh as some back then. This being said, I would emphasise that I have nothing but the highest respect for referees in all sports, let alone judo.

My career as a referee was quite short-lived as I was involved in some instances somewhat unbecoming of an official that included walking off the mat and inviting a member of the public complaining of my scores to come on to the mat and take over; I actually took off and offered him my jacket – shockingly, he declined. I was guilty of walking off a mat at Colchester when two players refused to accept my decision and a subsequent row with a coach where some coarse language was exchanged. Some guy produced a video actually confirming I got the verdict right but did I get any apology from either player or coach? Awarding a decision to the player who smiled at me at the end of the contest probably did not bode too well for a career as a referee either. I also recall at an event at Stowmarket in the days of decisions and line judges when we gave a split decision on a yuko. I signalled yuko from the mat, a corner judge of my level agreed but the other corner judge, a senior referee, signalled a higher score. Well, as you do, I ignored the dissenting view. At the end of the bout he got up and whispered in my ear I should have reverted to the opinion of the senior ref. I simply responded by pointing out we agreed 2-1 it was a yuko, he was wrong, and asked him to sit down. Yes, it was not received well. They were just a few of my scrapes, there were others.

I actually thought the club would only last a few years. Colin might get a National medal and his National flag, and we would all live happily ever after and I could finally head toward my middle-age beer belly. So we continued with the tournaments and both Charlotte and David were selected for the Junior Nationals at the end of 1994. The club was on a high as I had become British Veterans champion, our first-ever National gold, but sadly neither David nor Charlotte were able to take medals at their Nationals. During this period, sadly I found many of those who ran the Junior Nationals in the early 90s rude and officious and their arrogant manner as a whole certainly brought out the worst in me too; I will say I was certainly no angel either so I cannot be too critical. The question of what came first, the chicken or the egg, is still one to deliberate on. So much has improved over the years regarding the running of events in the UK.

We had finally gained recognition as a club and cracked the Junior Nationals but now the work on winning a medal really had to begin. I had no aspirations in these years of the Olympics for any member of the family, only sneaking a National medal or two.

The club was booming with players as we moved into 1995 and my focus was on Colin who was the player most likely to take a National medal. The financial strain of travelling the length and breadth of the country was taking its toll. Also I did not want to overexpose Colin on the circuit during his first National year. I had developed a mistrust of judo coaches in general, particularly outside the Eastern Area where the cut-throat nature of the game was at its worst. It seemed if you left a young player alone at matside, a rival judo coach would soon be chatting to them with promises of trips abroad and fantastic sessions at their club. They always insisted they had perfect sparring partners for them at their club. Indeed, to this day, this type of activity occurs; as recently as 2013 a coach was trying to encourage two of my more impressive girl players to his club in London with such promises at a competition in Southend.

Over the next ten years many players came through Kumo and became coaches with their own clubs and the advice I always gave them was not to expect any loyalty from a player unless they were your son or daughter. This being said, I have been very fortunate and have lost few players to the poachers and neither of the girls approached at Southend believed the bull being spouted either. Of course there is nothing wrong with players moving clubs if they feel there is a need; I, too, have had many players leave their clubs to join me, but, and it is a big but, I have never initiated that process. All players that have transferred to my club contacted me with that intent.

I recall a respected coach once telling my son Colin that he was wasting his time training at my club, being totally unaware who I was and that I was standing so close. Many years later it was delightful to see my son easily defeat his one. Strange how some words spoken can come back and bite you on the backside.

The video camera was now in its prime and was the new coaching tool. Often your player would be filmed and their style picked apart by a rival club, totally without your knowledge. In later years there would be some form of control exercised on filming at tournaments but even that idea went out of the window when some bright spark put a camera on a mobile phone and made monitoring this activity impossible.

My plan was to train Colin in private out of view and, with the benefit of my own hall, I embarked upon a series of closed events known as inter-club tournaments. The first of these tournaments had been organised a year earlier but someone had complained (yes, there are always complaints) that we had exceeded the BJA safety limit of 50. We had complied with the number rules and I was a little surprised that anyone would have bothered counting judo players with a view to making a complaint, it made little sense. I ran a series of closed competitions, many in private, often importing players for a specific purpose to meet the needs not just of Colin but of a number of promising young players. They were ideal in that they were on our doorstep and Denise, who was fast learning how to run competitions, could match our players according to their requirements. Colin was able to experiment with ideas on techniques and the result of the contest did not matter.

The powerful London club, Jodan, paid us a couple of visits and I built a lasting friendship with their coach Pete Salsbury, a brilliant coach who, in my view, was never given enough recognition by the BJA. It seems anyone without a record as a player in elite tournaments is not taken seriously. One day the penny might drop that elite player does not equal elite coach. Why is there that belief? Many, indeed most elite players seem to just disappear to another planet once they quit fighting. Pete produced wonderful players and some of those players he coached helped develop Colin, as many of them were in my son's group. Turan Kiani and Grant Eagleton were Pete Salsbury's players and Colin had many tough contests with each of them. Today they are now two very fine coaches following on in their coach's footsteps.

There was always bitter rivalry between Jodan and Kumo and we often gave each a great deal of stick at events but there was always a high level of friendship that never faded.

The first National event Colin was eligible for was the British Schools National. The British Schools Judo Association was not considered as tough as the BJA version but it was still a hard event. We travelled up to Cannock and Colin duly won his first National medal. It was a bronze, Colin only being beaten by a young Craig Fallon who went on to win countless honours.

As the year of 1995 drew to a close, the BJA Junior Nationals loomed ever closer. Colin's year had been a good one, while David and Charlotte had not performed so well and in all reality they could not have expected to be selected in that year (and were not), but Colin's selection was a formality. As a schools' medallist and given the countless medals won that year, what more did he need to do? Well the answer filtered back to me that he did not do enough big tournaments to merit selection. I was now getting seriously annoyed with this behaviour. It appeared the BSJA National bronze and medals at the Kent Open and many other London events did not count. Craig Peters had been selected. I appealed through the Area Committee via Stewart Collings and Colin was selected as number two to Craig Peters.

We received no paperwork about the event – we were just told to drop Colin off at Breckland Leisure Centre and he would board a coach for Crystal Palace that Friday night to fight the following day. It was all a shambles as far as I could see. Some years later, I learnt areas were issued with six passes for matside coaches but the area only allowed the chosen few which was two coaches between some 15 boy players and I was certainly not one of the chosen ones.

Not having been told of the start time of the event, and without the luxury of online calendars, we arrived just as Colin was walking off the mat from his opening contest. I was told by another parent he had won on a koka, a 3-point throw no longer recognised under the present rules. The area had a poor record of success at the Junior Nationals so not a lot was expected of any of the East's team but Colin battled through three more wins including a great win over the young Scottish player James Hare, which put him into the final and a medal as well as a British flag guarantee. Throughout the day no one sat in Colin's chair as his matside coach. Surely, I thought, in the final, one of the chosen few would be in his chair? Alas Colin fought the final alone and Gareth Carder, who would go on to be our friend and rival, ripped Colin to pieces with one stomach throw after another. A silver medal in our first National would surely signal the end of our problems within our area, one would think? Sadly not, so it was just building fuel to the fire. Colin was looking like the real thing and it was being made quite clear by some individuals in the East, that I was not the one to nurture this talent. Never did get that apology from anyone in the area for not selecting him in the first place.

The next National event was a BJA team event, which saw the Eastern Area boys' team win a silver medal at Crystal Palace in February. The only contest that Colin lost that day was to Gareth Carder yet again. Charlotte too represented the girls' team but they failed to reach the medal stages. I was still cautious of the set-up in the Eastern Area but we went with the flow. Colin had the matter of representing Great Britain at cadet level out in Venray but beforehand there was National squad training in Coventry with judo icon and double Olympic silver medallist Neil Adams. All was progressing nicely; the way forward seemed to have a clear pathway.

Colin, at the age of 12, duly travelled to Holland. It was very hard packing off a young son on to a huge coach with people you did not know, but we drove him down to High Wycombe and bid him goodbye. It would be the first of countless trips over the next 23 years with Great Britain which would see Colin travel to almost every part of the world. He had instructions to ring us as soon as he fought, and the day of the mobile phone had still not arrived so this would entail a 12-year-old getting to a public phone in a foreign country. We waited all day it seemed, until he finally rang, and informed us he got silver, losing to fellow Brit Chris Waddington in the final. In all truth the medal was more like a ceramic tile, more befitting being stuck on your bathroom wall rather than a trophy cabinet. The last time I remember seeing the thing, it was in my loft. What it looked like was not the issue. The club and Colin were on the move and that silver medal was Colin's first medal representing Great Britain.

There was something else on the move too. When Colin returned from Venray he was constantly requesting his back be scratched. Well, everyone likes a good old back scratch, but this became excessive. He was even doing monkey impressions rubbing his back up and down on the edge of a wall. Of course we told him to stop being stupid, until we took a closer look at Colin's back. A visit to the doctor confirmed he had scabies; in fact the whole family had scabies, and the back-scratching routine was becoming a family habit every night. Denise had the task of crossing the road to inform the mother of one of our players that her daughter was likely to have scabies as she often spent much time at our house, being one of Colin's friends. The treatment is to cover one's body, that is every part, with a liquid that burnt somewhat. I can confirm it burnt parts of the body that should not be burnt. All the bed sheets had to be washed and I am not too sure whether we were supposed to put a sign on the door spelling 'unclean'. Seriously, all that for a ceramic tile we could have bought from B&Q?

We embarked on another trip to Bavay with Kumuichi where, for the first time, I noticed the odd way that French junior players seemed to improve at an alarming rate after the age of 12 years old. Indeed, far quicker than those in the UK.

As the exchange scheme of accommodating players and parents became ever more difficult to organise the relationship between the clubs faded away.

Back in England the National cadet training was not what I expected. Whilst there is no doubting the ability of Neil Adams as a player and a coach, the Coventry mat was too crowded and there were no spectator facilities whatsoever, so it was difficult to see where progress was being made or even see the session at all. Parents and coaches simply could not fit into the hall. We had to hang around in the hallway for four or five hours. It made for one long boring day to add to a long boring drive, not the fault of Mr Adams but also not great for us wet-behind-the-ears parents either.

In May 1996 we travelled down to the Willesden International that was so 'International' it now had the unofficial title of the British Cadet Junior Open. Colin was in a massive group of some 36 players and battled through five wins to the final to meet what was rumoured to be a Hungarian Cadet champion. He had looked pretty awesome all day long and had battered all in his path to reach the last two. The final proved to be the classic all had expected, with Colin coming from behind to defeat the Hungarian with seconds to go. It was an indication of what was to come from Colin later in the year at the Junior Nationals. However, such is judo, we were brought back down to earth at the Kent International a month later by Gareth Carder, not for the first time, and had to settle for silver.

The Kumo Judo Club was also making an impression when we entered a recently affiliated Associations Championships in Great Yarmouth taking seven gold medals, two silver and eight bronze. Our club was producing a wide range of fine players and we were getting noticed for producing a range of good fighters.

Later in the year Colin took gold at the BSJA Nationals, David took bronze and I retained my British Veterans title for a third time, so the family haul of National medals continued to build up. It would be the last time I fought for a couple of years as the politics in the area gained momentum. The *Diss Express* continued to follow the club's results and the publicity was most welcome.

Within the Eastern Area, the squad managers had struck up a relationship with the North West Area and had arranged visits to Kendal and Bacup Judo Club for the elite of the area squad. Those elite did not involve any Kumo players, despite being one of the more prolific clubs, Colin included, but that was of little concern to me. The prospect of sleeping my son on a judo mat in a hall for a weekend camp and running up a hill with a Ford Cortina tyre on his back in the pouring rain (well it was the Lake District) at 12 years old could escape us as far as I was concerned. Eventually we were offered a spot but I was unhappy with the arrangements and declined it. There seemed to be no insurance cover for a venture like this with a parent using his own minibus for the trip; it was unacceptable to me. It was easy to see why parents would be keen for their children to do the camps; they were, as I understood the situation, very well run and they were packaged as Judo 2000, a kind of reference to the next Olympics in Sydney.

However, this was not the end of the issue as there was a rumour the Kendal camps may become part of the Area's selection criteria for the Junior Nationals. If you did not attend Kendal you were not going to be selected for the Junior Nationals. I was outraged; my son was one fight from the gold medal the previous year so why would I need to change anything? At this stage I would add it was not a case of believing that Kendal did not work, as for many players clearly it did. The Eastern Area medal haul nationwide was growing and there were a number of quality players emerging, no doubt as a result of the fine work done in the Lake District.

The point was I did not consider I needed any input from outside of my club. I was not interested in any intervention or input from other area coaches. What I was doing, had it been the wrong course, would only have compromised Colin's development and maybe that of other players in my club.

As regards training outdoors in freezing temperatures and driving rain and having to listen to such nonsense as 'having a cold shower will make a man of you'? That still makes my mind boggle.

There were cracks emerging between the Eastern Area committee and the squad managers, and Kumo Judo Club was between the two, so a kind of three-way tug of war on the issues of Kendal and area selections for the Junior Nationals was brewing. Looking back, I think those running Kendal had word of the fact that I opposed the sessions, and this simply was not true – I was simply protective of my son and I was of the view we did not need them.

What followed in the lead-up to the Junior Nationals in 1996 is still unclear (and frankly I simply was not interested in ever finding out what happened) but the area players attended the Nationals without the appointed squad managers being present. Again Colin fought without anyone matside or in his chair and, upon reaching the final for a second year, walked out to win a gold medal, without a coach, even though there were surplus coaching passes available to the East. The contest fought by Colin was, on my direction, looking back, somewhat disgraceful. Colin scored a 7-point score against Tom Smith and, from the crowd position, I yelled to simply run away for the last 20 or seconds and wind down the clock. The win was essential but, the way we achieved it, I would never be proud of. I never did get the opportunity to apologise for the method of victory to Tom or his parents but there were far-reaching reasons beyond just the medal as to why that win was of such paramount importance to me. The Eastern Area, in again failing to recognise I had a right to a matside coaching pass, was so dissappointing given how many coaching passes I knew they had. I could not allow my son to continually fight without a coach in his chair at what was the most important competition of the year. My thoughts were on the lines of how much else did I have to do to gain any recognition?

We tried lifting our profile as a club by awarding our players a club badge but on a tactical basis I found it was like putting a bullseye on the back of your player. At the time Pinewood was a massively successful club and all their players wore their club badge, however, even I had been guilty of saying to my players that they should not judge their development on winning medals but on whether you have beaten a Pinewood player that day. This created the scenario that my players gave everything against a player with a Pinewood badge and in the unlikely case they might have won came out for a final not really giving a hoot as to the result.

We ceased wearing badges after just a couple of years and to this day do not display our club on the judo suit nor do we parade in tracksuit tops. I came to the conclusion I would prefer to 'ghost' in and out of events. I am even opposed to the modern fashion whereby players have their names on their backs. At International events this is mandatory but when I see this on youngsters I do worry as if your player stands out it is easy for opposing coaches to track and identify them at competitions. There is that arguement that such a situation can only make your player better as your student has to continue to improve, not all would agree with me I accept.

As we approached 1997 it seemed the Eastern Area and the squad managers were back on track and looking to improve on the fantastic silver medal the boys' team had won in 96.

My views on holding trials for selection to attend Nationals were by now well known. I knew through Leigh Davies of the London system that it seemed less subjective than one person's opinion, where there is always a danger of bias. Had I not complained about Colin's non-selection in 1995 he would not have won a silver medal, so from my perspective it was clearly flawed.

In 1997 the area announced it would select players for the National teams based on trials, to be held at Breckland Leisure

Centre. It looked like I had got my way. Now, there used to be a saying in British judo, along the lines the British Judo Association will honour the results of the criteria set, provided they get the player they want. I am not sure if this was ever true, but certainly it is not so in today's BJA, where criteria are laid down and selections at all levels are transparent and clear, but in the mid-90s it is fair to say who you were, the contacts you had and those you may have socialised with could mean the difference between a player being left at home or fighting at an event. This applied at many levels. Players could be overlooked without apparent reason. Sadly the Area's trials would prove to be lacking in honour too.

The East's trials duly took place and one of my girl players, Gemma Calver, won her weight group beating her rival but was not selected. It was not even that Gemma was not successful on the circuit having won medals at some good quality events.

I was not given any reason for my player being overlooked.

Our reaction was to pull Colin out of the boys' team, resulting in a quarter-final 5-4 defeat (had Colin fought, the team would probably have won 5-4 and taken at least a bronze), and the girl who took my girl's place failed weight and had to fight up a weight anyway so my player could have fought. All Kumo players boycotted area events from that date, including squad training where the numbers fell drastically; our morale had sunk to new low. On a brighter note Colin claimed the gold at the Kent International, his main rival Gareth Carder moving up a weight.

At this point I had decided to quit work at Norwich Probate Sub-Registry, where I had been the chief clerk for some five years. To the shock of my former colleagues I became a part-time chicken sexer working just three to four mornings a week, which gave me the freedom to travel. Had I remained in an office job I would never have had the freedom to be available for the many jaunts across the world that lay before us and the taxi service I would provide for Colin's overseas trips with the British squad.

My later work as a chicken sexer would be a talking point at many a barbecue and, more to the point, Alan and Sheila Clark, who employed me, generously donated large sums (and I mean large sums) towards Kumo's overseas trips to the USA in the years to come. So there were added benefits too and not just for me, but the many children we were able to subsidise. Those years as a chicken sexer enabled me to devote most of my time to judo, leaving me free from midday onward. During the year, Denise had been steadily rising up the competition administration ladder but, in a bid to frustrate her progress, we received a letter from the BJA complaints commission stating we had fought players at a non-affiliated judo competition and as such had put them at risk, as their BJA licence would not cover their insurance. We were not allowed to know who made the complaint, which meant someone could hide behind the door and simply make trouble. Again I asked myself, why would anyone waste their life, following, it appeared, my every move in this minority sport? The allegations were also nonsense but it seemed, despite an explanation that we had dual licence holders on our mat (Amateur Judo Association (AJA) licence holders), which was within the rules as the AJA were affiliated to the BJA, Denise still received points on her licence.

We were all a little confused as to what was going on. To our knowledge we had not set out to offend or upset anyone or break any rules and yet we had been reported to the British Judo Association's complaints committee.

There seemed to be little point in carrying on in the sport. I knew Colin was a good player, but an Olympic prospect? The problem being we had some other National medal prospects in the club. As a family we decided we would quit totally after the Junior Nationals in November 1997, shut Kumo down and walk away from the sport altogether. We had to continue to the Nationals to repay the loyalty to our bunch of players who had remained solidly behind us.

By September we had transferred our licences to the London area so my players could fight and qualify for the Junior Nationals through a different area, one that used trials for selection, a fair system where an opinion would not be necessary. In doing so I was for the first time granted a matside coaching pass at the Nationals and at this stage Colin had already taken two medals for the East. We did not tell the East of our intentions to fight for London but, through one of my few contacts within the East, we heard that someone had boasted gleefully that Colin Oates would not be at the Nationals this year. I still cannot understand how anyone could have gained satisfaction from a statement that seemed to delight in the knowledge that a quality junior, a child, may be missing out on the premier junior event, simply because they had a problem with me. Was this an example of local prejudice just because we were originally Londoners? It summed up the attitudes of a number of individuals I had to contend with at that time; if they did not like the parent, targeting the offspring was, it seemed, fair game.

To this day I can still remember the stony silence as we walked past the East team at the weigh-in for the event. The following day the politics problems showed as Colin failed to reach a final, losing to David Lamb (the latter was the only player to ever beat Colin twice at the Junior Nationals and was never an opponent you wanted to draw at any stage of a competition). Still, a bronze medal was good enough and, at long last, courtesy of London, I had that hitherto elusive matside pass and could coach my children, unlike the previous years with the East. The following day it was the turn of my girls Gemma Calver and Michelle Brunning and what was to be our swansong event. Gemma was first up and battled out two wins against two losses in a pool of five and secured her bronze medal and a place in the Great Britain Cadet squad. My last task as a coach would be to help Michelle as far as I could. In a group of 14 players the task was a tough one but Michelle reached the semi-final, which she lost, and was left with a bronze medal fight. It was to be the last time I would sit in the matside chair for anyone, in some ways an emotive one for me. Nevertheless, the win was still vital to me and her. In a tense contest Michelle hung on to an earlier score to secure her place in the Great Britain squad and her first-ever bronze National medal.

What followed changed everything, as Michelle, a 14-year-old girl, walked off the mat and immediately cried on my shoulder at the end of the fight. Her mother told Denise that Michelle never cried. Such was the emotion of the moment, it meant that much to my players, all of whom had remained loyal to Kumo. It was at this point I realised these people would not drive us out. We would fight back against our opponents in the East and anyone else, until I obtained justice and fairness for all area players, but we had to carefully plan this and still protect Colin who clearly had been affected by the troubles of 97 in the area.

In 1998, with most players fighting on London licences, we rarely fought in the East; in fact it was my intention to fight less and less in the UK. By now I had realised that Europe was the key to development. I still had a referee ticket, Denise was well on the road to being a competition controller, which would mean we could, within BJA guidelines, run fund-raising competitions to provide a vital source of income.

That same year Denise stood at the Annual General Meeting for a place on the East's committee and was elected.

With Wymondham Judo Club, we started to organise higher-profile events like the South Norfolk tournament, which was one up from our inter-clubs, as practice for bigger events. Another trip with Kumuichi Judo Club to Hornu saw club members take part in an unusual team event which saw some of our girls having to fight French boys, and I watched in horror as our tiny tiger Taedi McLean conceded a koka (3-point score), then a yuko (5-point score) and then waza-ari (7-point score), only to see her then score the complete reverse of throws. A seven, then a five followed by a three, the difference being Taedi then ipponed him (a 10-point win). The poor French lad walked off the mat with his hands in the air in disbelief. Taedi was a tiny seven-year-old, not allowed to fight in Britain under the British Judo Association rules back then, so she had to gain her early experience in Europe. On the trip home Taedi insisted on going on the ferry's deck and I still remember having to cling on to her tightly for fear she might blow overboard; she turned into quite a character and is still friends with my daughter Vicky to this day.

The May Willesden International saw another five victories for Colin as he took yet another massive gold trophy at this magnificent event. A month later Colin won yet another bathroom tile, this time a bigger one, at the Venray International, winning five contests in a row; three weeks later at Crystal Palace five wins, and yet another gold at the Kent International. Although Colin was not the star of the show, that title going to his club colleague Zoe Kozlik, who in her bronze medal final had been thrown everywhere by her opponent and, with just two seconds remaining and trailing by four 5-point scores and a 7-score, Zoe secured a hold down and held out for the win. The father of the other girl stormed over towards me, and I must admit I thought, here we go again, more aggravation, but to my surprise he shook my hand and congratulated me on the fantastic performance of my player. He must have been gutted, it was a big medal, but that was sportsmanship of the highest order, a welcome change from what I had been experiencing.

October 1998 saw the first overseas event organised by Kumo. What an event! With 12 players in Holland we took just three medals; Colin took gold, Michelle Brunning silver and Taedi McLean a bronze. Our team was strong but Dutch junior judo is of a very high standard and we struggled. It was at this event I first met Willem De Korte. We travelled on the fast overseas ferry out of Harwich to Rotterdam, a service later withdrawn. The trip took just four hours but meant we arrived at midnight for what we described as a midnight meeting in Rotterdam with a Dutch guy. It sounded sinister and exciting, almost like a drugs deal. Sadly, I made a complete idiot of myself by walking over to shake hands with Willem without noticing a low chain fence. Not sure what Willem must have thought of this crazy Brit doing breakfalls in Rotterdam at midnight; all I remember is it really hurt my leg. The evening was much better as Willem and I shared lagers in the Sport Centre until the early hours while the team had sleeping-bag fights in the main hall. When we settled for the night in our sleeping bags in the dojo, many of the players had camped close to where I lay, but by morning they were at the farthest points of the hall. Apparently my snoring kept the arena awake and there was nowhere to hide despite the size of the hall; I recall sleeping quite well aided by Willem's beer. The overseas trips seemed the most positive way to develop players in an enjoyable climate and over the coming years there would be many more.

The end of 1998 saw Colin take another bronze at the Junior Nationals with Vicky, his younger sister, also taking bronze and a place in the British Cadet squad. By now we had four Great Britain Cadet internationals from our tiny village of North Lopham but the squad had grown in numbers, as they would now accept bronze medallists (not just gold and silver medallists as before) and guests were invited. The cost of the cadet squad overseas tournaments was quite high and I found we could do the same events for half the price. Moreover, junior players at the British Cadet squad sessions, especially some of Colin's rival players, would avoid working with him, especially a group of them from one particular club. I also watched as some of the parents chatted up the squad managers no doubt in the belief it would benefit their children.

The British Cadet squad managers at the time were excellent coaches and ran brilliant sessions but, just like the concept of the Kendal camps, I started to doubt whether we needed this at all. It was a lot of travel to the sessions and, in my view, unnecessary expense, money that could be used better in other ways. Moreover I had seen through my experiences with the French club, Bavay, how they developed better young players without this type of system (at least to my knowledge).

With the onset of 1999 the Eastern Area seemed to be more settled; there were still issues but they did not concern us. Unfortunately there was one final blow to the East we would inflict through the London area. The National team event was a tournament which brought the regional areas together and was a high profile event where the best from, say, the West would fight a team from London and so on.

My quality players fighting on London licenses were still in the London team drawn to fight the East with both Gemma Calver and Michelle Brunning in the line-up. Not only did we beat the East but we also medalled, so both my girls, neither of whom were considered good enough to represent the area they lived in, now added to their collection via a rival area. In many ways I was embarrassed for the guys from my area; it was never my intention to humiliate them in any way or interfere with what they were doing but I felt I had to represent my players and get what was best for them. I never wanted to walk away from the area I lived within.

In Groesbeck, Colin failed for the first time to win a medal overseas for the Great Britain Cadet squad, as he lost for bronze. I did not attend but I was given to understand from a father who was present that Colin did not have anyone in his chair for any of his fights, which sent out warning bells. On Colin's return from this trip he told me he overheard the squad managers talking about a funded trip to Florida and the team would consist of three players in my son's weight and age group. With Cadet Europeans and Youth Olympics on the horizon it did not take a Cambridge education to work out that Colin, despite his fine record, indeed better than most of those selected, was out in the cold.

The trip did take place, we lost out, and no, we were never a consideration for any cadet selections for major championships. A month later we trekked up to Gateshead to represent London at the National teams but did not progress.

In February the club had three successes at British Schools Judo trials to represent Great Britain at a massive tournament, once described as the World Schools Championships. Colin, Gemma Calver and Steven Flanagan all qualified as number ones in their weight group.

Sadly Gemma decided to decline her selection which left just Colin and Steven to fight in Belfort, France.

Denise and I travelled down with Bill Kelly, the Wolverhampton coach whose daughter was also fighting in the same competition. Bill did the entire drive, and quite how is beyond me. Somehow he managed to remain awake during the whole of the one-day return trip deep into France and back. Bearing in mind he had travelled down from the Midlands that day we owed him an enormous debt of gratitude.

Unfortunately, there was controversy. In those days the British Schools were not always on the ball, and on our arrival we discovered that you could only have two per weight category. Furthermore the weight category that Steven Flanagan had qualified for, that being under 50k, was not being fought at this event, but as number one in the British trials he was moved up to the next weight and was allowed to fight at -55k. Now Colin, being the number one and winner of the trials at -55k, should have been allowed to fight as the weight's top player, and only two could compete per weight category. However, the weight's number two James Lutman was allowed to stay in his natural weight whilst Colin was moved up to -60k where he was comprehensively slaughtered. I was so outraged I overruled the BSJA coaches and pulled him out after his first fight.

On our return I wrote a letter of complaint to the admin of the British Schools and withheld our final payment. What a brilliant response I got. A letter telling me my players had gone out that night and got drunk returning late, and threatening me with the complaints commission. It is a fact that if you receive a complaint and have no defence then one should go on the offensive and muddy the waters. I replied with the cheque and letter asking how these minors were allowed out and able to obtain alcohol but amazingly never did receive a reply. I actually banned the affiliations to the British Schools and no longer promoted anything to do with the organisation for many years. With the benefit of hindsight I should not have paid the balance for the trip either. Neither Colin nor Steven had drunk beer that weekend and indeed, throughout Colin's long career, he was never one to violate squad rules.

Back to Area politics, a meeting was held at my club with an official of the Eastern Area who shall remain nameless. He asked me to return my players to the East and told me, although he did not agree with area trials, if I came back there would be no reason why I could not introduce them if I stood for and got appointed as Eastern Area squad manager. This was too good an offer to refuse but on condition my players need not revert back from London until I was appointed. In truth it was the opening I needed, as fighting out of London was something of a strain because closed area events were off-limits to my players, which meant they had to constantly travel for competitions.

I duly applied for the boys' squad and was appointed following an interview and, as no one applied for the girls, was subsequently appointed their interim manager. During the interview it was clear that one of the selection panel did not want me appointed and asked the question of how I would feel if an Eastern Area player was drawn against one of my London registered players? Whose side would I be on? At this time Udo Quellmalz was the Great Britain squad manager, so my reply was easy, and I responded by saying I would feel exactly the same as our German manager would feel if a British player was drawn against a German player at the European Championships. I later heard I got the appointment on a 2-1 split vote, no surprise in that. I only needed one guess to work out who was the one that opposed me but that is politics and to this day I do not bear any grudge to that individual or any other who had passionate beliefs on the best way forward that may have disagreed with mine.

While all of this was going on we had not lost sight of judo, as we had probably our finest hour in organising an overseas tournament in Philadelphia, USA, with 11 children. I warmed up, winning the Southern Area Veterans Championship in Aldershot; in truth I only needed to win a couple of contests to take gold. During our stay we arranged for all the children to attend schools and stay with American families.

This trip even caught the attention of Anglia TV. We had a camera crew visit our club. It was my first-ever TV appearance, as I refused to count the back of my head pictured on the *Big Match* at Charlton v Derby in 1968. They spent nearly two hours at the club doing the interviews. They started with me and I was given a dress rehearsal of five questions, all of which I answered quite brilliantly. Then the camera rolled and I answered everything differently; there is no accounting for human stupidity, especially my own. Colin and Vicky were brilliant and Anglia TV used those clips many years later in a programme prior to the London Games.

Thanks to a sponsor (Alan and Sheila Clark, my employers as a chicken sexer), the kids had a free trip to New York and a visit up the Empire State Building. The Liberty Bell tournament still runs today and remains one of America's biggest judo tournaments. Taking off from Heathrow on a Virgin Atlantic 747 jet was something else. With so many children to look after for a week or so, there were issues like: what if one of them gets seriously ill, what would I do? Looking back I must have been crazy to take all of those children.

On the aircraft, one of the girls in my group was busily complimenting me on how I had sweet-talked the headmistress of St Andrews School in North Lopham by telling her that I had arranged for all the children on the flight to attend American schools. She seemed quite horrified when I told her that I was not conning her headmistress and they would truly attend school during their stay. It was of course an experience of a lifetime and they all enjoyed their trips to school.

We brought back many friendships from the USA that have lasted to this day. It was at this event I met the USA's team manager Lou Moyerman; in fact, Denise and I stayed with him for a week.

He was an amazing character, totally dedicated and willing to arrange transportation from Newark airport to Philadelphia for all my party. I remember him filling up his MPV with 'gas', as they say, and Denise asked if I should make a contribution to the cost. To my surprise the gas was a quarter of the price it was in the UK; I thought it might have been an insult so did not say anything.

Lou was a teacher at Fells High School and, while all the Kumo children had been packed off to the lower schools in and around Philadelphia, we attended a lesson Lou was giving. The lesson was titled, 'What drug I would design and the effects it would have on me.' Somewhat different to a lesson on Shakespeare I thought. Amazingly it fitted the genre of the class, except an enormous young lad, built like a tank and looking real mean who slept with his head in his arms the whole lesson. We sat and waited for Lou to explode at him but nothing happened. At the end of the lesson Lou came over and asked my views. I told him it was an excellent lesson as he had a class of difficult young people all interested, but asked about the sleeping guy in the corner. Lou said, and I quote, 'Part of his parole is to attend High School, why did you wanna wake him?' I took on board his viewpoint and agreed he could sleep as long as he wanted to, given the size of this guy. I would even have offered him a blanket and pillow.

We took just five medals from a team of 13 players, with Colin's gold medal victory over Taraje Williams Murray (who went on to be a double US Olympian just like Colin) the highlight of the judo. I took silver and in doing so discovered a very different competition system whereby if you lost the final, as I did, it is necessary to defend your silver status against the other repechage player. Before my silver fight-off, my 15-year-old son Colin gave me instructions on how to beat my opponent, which worked and very quickly. I had already beaten this player but it was a very tough majority-decision verdict. When this man found out I had taken advice on how to beat him from a kid, he went off rambling about getting beat by a 15-year-old British kid. In truth I think I might well have lost otherwise, as the earlier fight was so hard. On Colin's advice I threw him for a full 10-point score; even at this young age Colin was showing a maturity far beyond his years.

During our stay my American friends decided to take Denise and I out to a bar, which seemed like a good idea – yet more of real-life America. That was, of course, until we arrived at O Shays Irish Bar. To add insult to injury it was also St Patrick's Day. The ink had hardly dried on the Good Friday Agreement. When I expressed my reservations as a Brit on entering the bar (at that time there was still considerable strife in Ireland), their response was, and I quote, 'Man, they don't even know where Ireland is.'

In American bars, they have a system of serving beer by the bucket (jugs), and it seemed my newfound buddies were intent on getting us all somewhat 'ratted'. Now American beer on tap is not the strongest and this is why Mexican Corona and stuff like that is popular, so this process was not going to take one or two buckets, perhaps five or six would be heading in the right direction. Maybe it is time to be honest about American beer and admit it would probably have taken a bathtub to have any effect on me. Anyhow, drinking buckets rather than pints invariably means you are flushing your system thoroughly and visits to the toilet would be frequent.

On one trip I encountered a gentleman who was talking to me, I think trying to flog me cannabis; I can't be sure because the word he was using has two meanings and can mean simply going to the toilet and, given where we were … I do love the USA and Americans but I have real difficulty understanding some of their accents. In all honesty I never really knew what the hell this guy was talking about so I smiled sweetly and went back for another bucket. That was one visit; the next trip to the toilet was even better. Now when I say I was drinking buckets, it is fair to say it takes a long time to discharge the contents of one or two buckets of beer from your bladder. In fact, so long that an early morning brawl had taken place in the bar (well, it was an Irish bar) in the time it took for me to process American beer. At about four in the morning we decided to leave, and one of the Americans staggered out totally incapable of walking in a straight line. To my amazement he got into his car, mumbling he had to start work at six; his mate reassured me that he drove better when he had a few. I do not know to this day how Denise and I got home as I still do not know where we had even been that night.

I am not sure what part of the visit was most enjoyable – the judo, the school experience or being introduced to Philadelphia Cheese Steak. Certainly the trip to the Irish bar ranks up there too. It is a close call but I think the Philly Cheese Steak might just win. Many years later Sean Pettit, our token American as we describe him at our judo club, would ensure I would have a ready supply of Philly Cheese Steaks at our summer barbecues.

The whole visit was a wonderful insight into the real USA, even being asked by a young American player to slow down when I spoke to him because he could not understand my accent (really??). Denise and I met up again with Lou at the World

Championships in Birmingham that year (1999) when Jimmy Pedro took gold. I still remember holding that medal that evening and, although I am sure Mr Pedro will never remember me, I was an avid supporter of him from that day. He was a real gentleman. On that same day I recall watching a young English lad called Danny Kingston, in my view being robbed in an early round, little realising he would, within the next 20 years, be living in the next village to us.

By 1999 one would have expected the high school Colin attended to be singing the praises of a judo player that had taken National titles and medals, but as usual many schools have a tunnel vision of just believing sport revolves around football and rugby. Colin had the misfortune of attending the same school as the Premiership footballer Matthew Upson, so judo took very much a back seat at Diss High School. On the contrary, the village primary school, St Andrews, under a succession of headships during the 90s, was very supportive and such support is still evident to this day.

The age of the internet was still a little way off and finding overseas events still proved hard. I once asked someone I thought was a friend (that happens quite a lot in this game) how you get overseas tournaments, to which he replied, in a rather unhelpful manner, that you have to work at it. I knew he had access to many but clearly he was not prepared to share them. Work at it we did and what would follow over the next 12 years would be unprecedented in the eastern counties with trip after trip.

Just a month after returning from the USA we travelled to Belgium for the Brussels International where Colin took gold, as team-mates and fellow GB Cadet players Michelle Brunning and Gemma Calver took silver and bronze respectively. In May a trip to Genval and yet another gold for Colin; it was beginning to appear as if he was unbeatable in Europe and I have to admit I started to believe he was one of the top juniors on the continent. I was totally unaware of the talent brewing in Holland, France and Germany, to name but a few.

Sister Vicky made her one and only appearance as a Great Britain Cadet in Venray, losing both contests, and finding out that, although she had been born in a town, she was very much a country girl in the company of city girls with very different attitudes to life.

The club was now dominant in the East Anglia region and entered 16 players at the Samantha Blake Memorial tournament in Great Yarmouth where we won our first trophy as a club, topping the medal table. My finest moment in Britain came when I won the -66k British Masters at High Wycombe in September, winning all four contests en route to my 3rd Dan. How strange, no matter how many medals you win, the one memory that never fades is winning a Dan grade. I managed to throw Dave Saunders with an Uchi Mata for those final points, which was a special moment; no mean feat as he was a good player and had beaten me many times before.

On 26 October 1999, as Eastern Area girls' and boys' squad manager, I held the first real trial for players, at Breckland Leisure Centre, who wished to attend the British Cadet Championships. Honestly, I really could not believe the response. I was told by Area coaches that players who were not up to it would automatically get selected if they qualified through the trials system. If they were injured I would be liable and the Area's reputation would be at risk.

For the first time in the East's history I had created a transparent selection system, and I was being castigated as an idiot and called far worse names by some of the Area's coaches. Again, without wishing to labour a point, what did it matter? This was just another tournament; okay, the odd decent player would be there, but that player could meet them at any event and indeed injure one from our neck of the woods at a lower level competition. I actually had the power to select exactly who I wanted so I could have scrapped the trials and selected just my own club players, but sometimes, when you see what you consider a lacking in reason or compromise in people, it can, as in my case, make you more stubborn. This whole dispute was pointless.

There were two more trips to Holland in October; Colin took silver in Hoogvliet and gold in Chitari a couple of weeks later.

The Junior Nationals were something of a personal disaster as Colin only took bronze as did sister Vicky, but in my first year as Eastern Area squad manager we had hauled a record 11 medals, a feat never before achieved and, even until the present time, not equalled. Newly acquired Samantha Peters was the star of the Kumo show taking a gold medal and becoming British champion following one of the most nail-biting finals I have ever sat through. Despite this showing, there were calls for an inquest from Eastern Area coaches as to what went wrong.

THE OVERSEAS YEARS
2000–2004

AS THE area squad manager, one of the first matters I had attended to was the stripping of mine or any future squad manager's powers. I announced through the Area newsletter that squad sessions would no longer be mandatory, as previously, to gain selection for the Junior Nationals. I put in place a date for future trials and also announced I did not want an influx of players from other clubs attending my club nights as had often happened to previous managers in the past. In addition to damaging club numbers if you lost your appointment as manager, those players would move on to another club after decimating your homegrown players, many of whom may have been non-competitive but nonetheless battered off the mat by the incoming hordes.

So there was a selfish motive there, being the protection of my Kumo club, which by now had become one of the more prolific clubs in the area. I was still hearing on the grapevine that the three top coaches in the East disagreed with my trials and many other matters. To this day I am unsure who they were supposed to be, as few coaches travelled like I did, so I put it down to just more backhanded insults towards me, which was not unusual. When I think of it they were saying I was not even one of the three better coaches in the East. There were also rumblings in the East that Colin was not that good, merely well managed. Probably a reference to the fact that I often moved Colin up and down the weights, often to dodge a player I did not want Colin to fight at that time. I had seen first-hand at the GB squad how some of Colin's rivals avoided training with him so it was they who drew the battlelines on the tactics front first and not me.

Without the worry of Junior Nationals selection I could now concentrate on the real task in hand, that of coaching judo. The year of 99 had proved to be a good one with four overseas trips and, through the trials, a selection of some 40 Eastern Area players for the Junior Nationals with a record return of 11 medals, a record for the East. There were the usual moans and groans from some of the Area's die-hard coaches saying I sent players not up to the task, but to my mind a 25 per cent return justified my decision to send all who qualified.

We managed to salvage a cadet team for the National Teams Championship at Crystal Palace where the East, thanks to six of the seven wins coming from a village hall club in the middle of nowhere, actually defeated a country, Wales, 7-4. Our luck ran out against the Northern Home Counties who beat us 1-9 and then defeat against the West eliminated us.

As the Nationals approached, we entertained the Belgian club Kemzeke in Norfolk as preparation for the Kumo players. I was introduced to the club through Leigh Davies and I initially contacted their secretary with a view to going to Belgium. However, the tables were turned when they wrote back and told me they wanted to come to Britain. You might have expected a minibus or a couple of carloads? I was presented with a 52-seat busload. Where could I accommodate this lot, I wondered? The answer was our village hall. We took over the hall for the weekend and I contracted a fish and chip van to feed them – back then there was none of this healthy-eating nonsense. We took them to the Kings Head Pub in North Lopham on the Saturday late afternoon, an evening that turned into a Sunday morning and telephone complaints from the local residents about the noise. The publican later told me that, in his 20 years behind the bar, he had never taken so much money.

The following day at the friendly competition Colin and David both impressed the Belgian team coach, so much so he asked if both would fight in the Belgian league for them. I thought it was a joke but accepted the offer. To my amazement more coaches emerged from the bus seemingly excited by the prospect. What followed was a link to this day with this club with many more Kumo players benefiting from fighting in the Belgian league. It turned out to be the perfect transition for a junior player, fighting in an adult league with divisions. As Kemzeke were in a lower league division at the time, the standard of adult player was far lower than the harsh ranking events in Britain where National squad seniors often competed. The relationship between our two clubs has now spanned over 20 years.

Trips to Belgium in June for two competitions in one weekend saw newly crowned British champion Samantha Peters and Taedi McLean rack up 11 wins between them as they took double gold, with Vicky Oates taking gold and silver. The strength in depth of the club was now not in any doubt. That weekend our players took ten gold, three silver and seven bronze medals, with us just nine players and this was without Colin or David Oates.

In October, both Colin and David debuted in the Belgian league, winning all the contests, as they began the transition into senior judo and attracting overseas television coverage for the first time. That was an amazing experience – to see a Flemish commentary about my two sons.

At the Junior Nationals, Colin took gold with five great wins. Without my concerns over selections for the Nationals, Colin was back to his best. It had become clear, however, that Colin had been targeted by a particular club where there were rival players in his category. Such players seemed to be drilled in how to stifle Colin's judo. One coach in particular was constantly heard yelling 'hold his leg' – well, actually what I used to hear was, 'old eees lig', but I think I interpreted it okay as I did once see an episode of *EastEnders*) – at this time you could often get away with leg grabbing – and before anyone complains about my sending up of a cockney accent I was born in Canning Town, and these Londoners were my mates. This was the normal method of stifle employed, penalties for leg grabs were still some way off. We needed to take Colin out of the English circuit and hide him, but at this level it would be difficult. We, as a family, were not enjoying the English competitions anyway, where it was easy to predict who you would be fighting, we needed variety of styles. The British opposition knew exactly how Colin would fight and their coaches usually had a game plan to combat his techniques which often prevented us developing new throws. The closed door inter-club competitions we had been running were fine at the lower end but we now needed more.

Taking yet another big Area squad to the Junior Nationals was an eye-opener. Being responsible for someone else's offspring is some burden. All the hotel rooms had to be checked before we left and many were in a deplorable state as a result of the children we were looking after. One in particular still had the bathwater left with towels just thrown in and water running. The task of being an Area squad coach seemed to reach far beyond that of just being a coach and it seemed one needed to be a minibus driver and almost a foster parent to the many children. I had to content myself with the belief that not all parents had the flexibility that I had and certainly not the crazy dedication that was required.

Following Colin's performance at the Junior Nationals, his first gold for three years, I thought it right and proper to maintain his high and, although he was eligible for the British Youth Trials, I decided the right thing to do for his mental development was to sit on the glory. I did not want to over-expose him to the British any more than I had to. We went to Wolverhampton in December with Vicky, who reached the second stage and went out; Sam Webb (who eventually married my oldest daughter) losing for bronze, and Samantha Peters, who according to the officials lost both her fights. The decisions in some really close fights that went against her that day probably robbed British judo of a future Olympian and left very deep scars with her. Whilst loath to criticise the decisions that cost her that day she really did have a tough time. Samantha carried on fighting for just a few more months but her heart simply was not in the sport anymore.

The turn of the new century saw Kumo step up the overseas missions with what turned out to be our final trip to date to the Liberty Bell tournament in the USA, at least as a club. An even bigger return of medals resulted, but this time Colin got beaten in the final. Our tiny tiger Taedi McLean clung desperately to a yuko (5 points) win to become our youngest Liberty Bell medallist ever when taking a bronze at the age of eight. At a meeting a few years later it was said by a coach that this girl was not fit to go to the Junior Nationals as she was likely to be overwhelmed by the occasion. This problem with the selection by trials just did not fade away. Our tiny tiger had fought in Europe and the USA many times and was so laid-back I could have fought her in front of 10,000 spectators and it would not have bothered her. Again did it matter? This girl fulfilled the criteria for attending the Nationals set by the governing body so was eligible.

The judo highlight had to be our British Junior champion Samantha Peters, who cruised to a great gold medal by winning three cracking contests. It was clear the trips across the Atlantic, whilst great for the kids and the club, were not where we were likely to improve our judo.

Judo in the USA is surprisingly not very popular and when they do get good players more often than not one of them would live in New York and the other in Los Angeles – miles apart and this causes no end of issues obtaining training partners of quality. Many of my American friends have often told me how lucky we are to live in Europe with so much quality across the Channel. My attentions had to be focused in Europe.

On this visit we stayed at a hotel where, to save money, we housed six to a room. Whilst checking in, I told the kids to keep moving in and out of the hotel foyer so that the hotel staff would not be able to count how many of us there were. Not ideal, health and safety would have had kittens, but yet again the kids got real value for money, including a tour of New York as part of the package we put together, which included a coach trip that brought us past the World Trade center. From the window of the coach it was impossible to see the top of the towers.

The morning after, we heard gunshots outside the hotel, which turned out to be a shooting of a man attempting to steal a vehicle; we learnt he was killed but fortunately our party only heard the incident and was spared the view.

Whilst at the hotel, the Kumo club, it seemed, was trying to emulate a heavy rock band by being noisy and generally anti-social. It is not easy to keep so many excited and jet-lagged kids quiet. One of my players, an 18-year-old, Sam Webb, who became my son-in-law, had a face-off eyeball to eyeball row in the corridor with an American business woman, and the situation was not helped by my American friends deciding to turn up at the hotel armed with countless crates of a Mexican beer I had not seen before. It was my first taste of Corona and certainly not my last. Sadly, things got carried away and complaints rolled in from other people staying at the hotel about the noise levels, resulting in the security threatening to kick us out. I have very vivid memories of staring at the security guard's big shiny badge and more alarming ones about his gun. Fortunately they loved my accent and I was able to blame my native buddies for the commotion, so we were spared trying to make arrangements to go across the street to a hotel that looked too much like the Bates motel from the Hitchcock film *Psycho*.

On our check-out, the hotel tried to charge me extra for the hire of a couple of films one would not be expecting the younger generation to be viewing, but when I asked why minors could be allowed access to these channels they quickly removed them from the bill. Never did get to the bottom of who had put those on. The final trip to Philadelphia holds special memories as we flew past the ill-fated twin towers on our way out of Newark airport that night, all of us oblivious to the horrors that would beset them just 18 months later. The aircraft dimmed its lights as it passed over New York and to this day I remember staring down at the New York skyline and the lights of those magnificent skyscrapers. It was a moment to remember and made the event of 9/11 somehow closer to home than the real distance between Norfolk and New York.

The early years of the new millennium saw the age of communication really taking off with more and more people possessing mobile phones the size of a house brick and only capable of ringing another number, whilst the video camera was equally shrinking in size. Little did we know the video camera would eventually shrink into the mobile phone which itself would reduce such technology to a quarter of the size. The onset of the computer age was also gathering momentum and the e-mail, in addition to replacing the letter, was a new weapon of war, used for saying something to someone without actually confronting them face to face. As far as Eastern Area personality differences were concerned a new tool could be used to criticise or insult someone and share that experience with 50 or so other recipients.

I still had lots of opposition to my decision to introduce trials within the area and the internet was the final attack. We labelled them 'the E-Mail wars'. Many of them were actually funny. We often sat laughing at the abuse being bandied around the area, far better than watching the television. It appealed to my sense of humour, especially when someone wrote something in all innocence only to be mauled online before a multitude of other readers, most of whom you would never have known and I am sure had no idea what the e-mail was about either.

We, Charlotte and myself, held meetings with other Eastern Area coaches to resolve issues, such were the feelings about my changes in squad matters, but there was no compromise. They would not budge an inch and neither would I, especially when it came to squad selection; they still wanted to revert back to subjective selections, and here I was sitting on the power over their players. I had introduced trials and they would stay as long as I was in control and, with the ever-growing presence of Kumo personnel on the Area Committee, there were few ways anyone could oppose us. At the end of the day we, as a family, often wondered (and still do), what the big deal was over the selections for the Junior Nationals, as looking back it was hardly likely to make headline news. It was so pathetic, given that a few years later the BJA opened the Cadet/Junior Nationals so that players could enter without their area's nomination. In essence I was years ahead of my time in effectively allowing Eastern Area players to enter the Junior Nationals if they so wished provided they met the grading criteria set by British Judo. For many players the old selection criteria had caused much grief; some players, my own included, had defected to other areas in search of fairness and openness.

There was one last shot individuals in the East were about to launch against my tenure as Eastern Area squad manager and that was reference to the area's constitution that I should be a senior club coach. At the time I was just a club coach so I registered for an area coaching course in Thetford, but it was clear I was being messed around, even delayed, and it seemed to be a deliberate ploy to get rid of me as squad manager. I simply completed the course in the London Area and again removed any further control that any of my opponents had over me. Eventually the Eastern Area would refund my course fee which in no way covered my costs in obtaining the qualification in London but I did what was necessary to represent not just my players but now as the Area squad manager those within Norfolk, Suffolk and Cambridge to the full.

The following years did mean we could just concentrate on the judo and 2000 was the beginning of Colin's real development. We had to look at the transition of Colin moving from a junior player to a senior player.

With the internet, it became easier to find and contact overseas clubs and competitions. I was once told I had to work at getting such events by a less than helpful individual and this I did. We rattled off trip after trip to the Benelux countries where we were able to take many children from the club courtesy of a cheap minibus supplied by Colgate of Diss. I once took a Colgate minibus to Belgium without filling in any paperwork and on returning the bus the manager told me he would not charge me as they had not missed it over the weekend. I insisted I leave some money and he reluctantly took just £10. Without their kind support the trips would not have been so plentiful. Colin could now fight and develop without being stifled by opponents in the UK well prepared for his style and a number of gold medals were won as a result with valuable experience gained.

It was not all good as Colin's first crack at gaining entry into the youth squad failed down in Bristol when he was eliminated. One of those days when everything that could go wrong or against you did and would, perhaps not for the first time. This would only amplify that the only way to guarantee the win is to be the better player on the mat without any shadow of a doubt. It is often all too easy to blame the officials on losses rather than your own coaching and I think I was beginning to realise perhaps I had misread many a situation with officials. There really is no substitute for experience.

At this time we had ceased attendance at cadet squad as we had considered it a waste of financial resources and time and had decided to travel to tournaments overseas ourselves. It was cheaper and I was in more control in selecting what I

A six-year-
old Colin in
his first ever
competition at
Abbs Cross School
Hornchurch.

Colin chases his
opponent.

That first ever
competition win
is close.

An eight-year-old Colin proudly poses with his first two judo medals.

The five fighting members of the Oates family in 1992 now included Charlotte, Vicky, David, Colin and Howard.

Colin in his first overseas competition, taking a silver medal out of Bavay.

Howard winning an overseas silver medal in France to equal Colin's earlier performance

North Lopham's finest – Gemma Calver, Colin and Michelle Brunning showing off their Great Britain cadet badges in 1997.

Howard Oates presents a trophy to host Lou Moyerman to thank him for his wonderful hospitality during the club visit in 1999.

Kumo players prepare for a tough training session at the Liberty Bell Judo Club.

Gemma Calver poses with her finest medal at the Liberty Bell judo competition.

USA judo legend and double Olympic medallist Jimmy Pedro presents Colin with his medal.

After the competition – time to play in the Philadelphia snow.

The crazy concept of building a dojo in a back garden takes shape in preparation for the World Championships in Egypt.

Job nicely done.

An injured David had to be content to sit out the camp in Budapest and play cards with his brother.

The customary camel ride with Vicky celebrating her 18th birthday in the Egyptian desert.

David, Emma and Colin sampling the heat of the May sunshine in Lausanne following the Swiss Open.

David pictured with his Irish Senior Open gold medal in Dublin in 2007.

Colin poses with his family just before his Commonwealth Games Final in 2014.

considered to be beneficial to Colin's development or indeed any other player within the club. It also meant my players had a coach in their chair which I had been told was not always the case. It was clear to see who was likely to get selected for the Youth Olympics and the European Cadet Championships, so it would have been helpful to make the youth squad where all expenses were paid and overseas trips were free to compensate for the fact we had no future so far as the cadets were concerned, but not everything goes your way.

The second Eastern Area team I had led to the Junior Nationals came back with another major haul of medals, Colin's gold being one of ten won by Area players (now 21 medals in two years) including Colin's sister Vicky, who by now had decided she would not fight again for the British Cadet squad. She had not enjoyed the experience of overseas travel with the squad and relative strangers; in fact she hated the idea of travelling without her club. We could visit any of these tournaments as a club at far less cost and it would be more enjoyable as the team all trained with each other and were mates. Vicky would carry on competing for some years to come but had no intention to aspire to any great heights even though she was an excellent player and held victories over many girls who went on to senior squad level.

At this stage Colin was 17 and I had to look to his future outside of judo. I told both David and Colin that I would financially support their judo as long as they obtained degrees before they were 21 years old. In David's case it was evident he may struggle to make an elite player; at this point his only National medals were from the Schools. Although now quite successful on the circuit he had not performed too well at major events as a junior. In Colin's case it was vital he would have a backup plan in case of injury or if he simply did not get there. I was well aware that a top judo player is quickly dropped and forgotten once their form fades or age catches up with them. In truth the only target I had was a B Tournament medal, nowadays referred to as a European Cup. Hopes and aspirations of anything further were still beyond my thinking.

There was the additional issue of the dreaded transition of a junior player into a senior player. By 2000 many of the children who had been our rivals had faded away from the sport but for those that did not they had the harsh senior ranking circuit to contend with. The BJA ran some ten events a year through the Area structure whereby medallists obtained ranking points and places in the top ten of Britain. These events were serious as the top four obtained entry into the Great Britain senior squad. In 2000 Colin and David were still effectively boys but we had the option of fighting in Division Four of the Belgian team league with Kemzeke. This seemed an ideal transition – a low-level event and senior players that would not be taking judo too seriously.

We had travelled to Antwerp in October and December to compete for Kemzeke, which proved a huge success, winning promotion to Division Three and both brothers now often featured on Belgian television. The league still remains a special event with an atmosphere that is amazing. Colin and David won all their contests and became a permanent fixture in the team.

Back in the UK, Kumo found itself homeless. The club had operated out of Garboldisham Village Hall for some six years and we had supplied letters to the hall's committee to assist their grant application, which they had been struggling to obtain prior to us renting the hall. A new hall was proposed but we were promised this would be built alongside the old one and we could have a smooth move from one to the other. This never came to fruition; the old hall was to be demolished and we were effectively homeless with a booming judo club full of players winning National medals and just a few weeks to find a home. The bottom line being, our use in supplying letters to obtain grants for the build was no longer required.

As luck would have it, the hall at Lopham was available and the stage, originally an obstacle, had been removed. Again I was told they would need letters from me to assist in grant applications for hall improvements but the committee promised our sessions would not be interfered with. The Lopham Village Hall committee kept their promise and the club still continues to thrive in the hall with the support of the village to this day. How pleasant it was to find a village hall committee that acted with honesty.

With the future of Kumo's main base secured, we could continue Colin's development as a player. We had started various satellite clubs at Botesdale and Debenham and we ran sessions at local schools to boost club funds necessary to continue our overseas campaigns.

Medals were now rolling in for both Colin and David, with youngest sister Vicky looking very promising too. Charlotte had never truly recovered from the treatment she received at an area grading where we all felt she was denied her opportunity to fight for her black belt a few years earlier. Slowly but surely she faded away from the sport. She continued to assist the club and area at competitions. She only ever rarely fought beyond 2001.

Both Colin and David were, by 2001, studying for degrees, David in Business Studies and Colin in Sports Science. As they were at commutable colleges they could continue training at the Kumo Judo Club. With the benefit of hindsight, perhaps the step back in 2000 from high-level judo (not entering the Youth Trials) was a mistake, but with our involvement in the Belgian league and some three visits a year to Antwerp in addition to our overseas club visits we were still able to continue our transition from junior player to adult.

As with any father, perhaps there was part of me that did not want to put Colin to the test. I suppose it could be said that by doing overseas tournaments we had run away from some of the domestic opponents. The truth was that, by 2001 I had first-hand experience of how nasty and two-faced some of the coaches could be; moreover, the behaviour of some of the parents was also deplorable. This is not to say that I was an angel either. In what can, in Britain, be described as very much a minority sport I had encountered much bitterness, especially at local level. Hearing people you once considered friends, as was now occurring, cheering on Colin's opponents regardless of whether they had a connection with that opponent or not is, to say the least, quite upsetting.

In later years I would advise all my children's parents to totally ignore the parents of their children's opponents at competitions and not to get too friendly as it would usually end badly. There is in my view a misguided belief that you can keep the situation on an even keel but I doubt human nature has greatly changed over the years. Listening to a big cheer from those people once thought of as friends every time your son loses is difficult. Whatever the differences with me it had nothing to do with my son. It was in essence little wonder over the coming years Colin would fight less and less in the UK and by 2001 we were also training exclusively at Kumo and did not visit any other clubs, nor did we entertain any visitors to the club. We had by now isolated ourselves.

In a bid to fight occasionally in the UK we took out Amateur Judo Association licences in order to compete in the AJA Nationals in Birmingham. The AJA had by then affiliated to the BJA so no one could grass us up for being involved in two associations. Charlotte and Colin were duly crowned 'British champions' as one would have expected. My daughter Vicky, the eternal rebel, battled to the final against a girl who was clearly the local favourite. Before the contest Vicky received what had to be a vital call on the mobile and stood at the side of the mat with the phone in her ear whilst the referee was frantically waving them on to the mat. She then defeated her opponent, walked off the mat, picked up the phone and started back on her conversation with a very patient caller on the other end. One of those moments where, as a father, not just as a coach, you want the ground to open up and swallow you. In AJA events, matside coaching has never been allowed so I was able to snake away unnoticed I think.

We travelled to an event called the Brussels under-23s on April Fools' Day and how right that turned out to be. We arrived for the weigh-in at nine in the morning and Colin and David were called to fight at half past seven in the evening. The event must have been oversubscribed three times over and to add insult to injury we came back without any medals. Many years later at Eastern Area-run events I would often have to listen to irate parents moaning that their kid had been at the event for two hours and had yet to fight; needless to say I usually have little sympathy and take great delight in boring them with tales of our hanging around in Europe. They usually walk away sorry they raised the issue.

On our way to Belgium we had a puncture on the M20. To my horror I found that my spare was also flat so I called out our rescue who told me there would be a charge because I did not have a serviceable spare wheel. When the guy arrived he found my electric air pump in the boot and pumped up my wheel and put it on the car. Within a week I got a bill for £70 for them using my pump to inflate my wheel. In the modern day, cars do not even have a spare wheel.

In May 2001 Colin defeated brother David in the final of a tournament in Marcinelle, Belgium prompting the question from the tournament organiser, 'Are you brothers?' Well, they have never really looked alike but the surname might have been a hint. On a positive note they were becoming the main rivals to each other even in overseas events.

I felt it was time to chase down the Junior World and European Judo Championships. To achieve this end we had to win a place on the youth squad. There were some good players on the circuit at that time and this would be a challenge.

The Youth Trials were held in Gateshead in December 2001 and did not go very well for Colin. There was a group of 30 players in his weight category and there were some very capable young players too. The trials were held on a pool on pool basis and, although Colin lost two fights that day (yet again to David Lamb who always proved to be an opponent you preferred to avoid), he found himself with just a bronze medal. It meant we had an uphill battle to get the number one spot and a crack at the Junior Worlds or Europeans later in 2002. Oddly, of the 18 categories fought that day, not one of those young players who won gold medals would go on to represent Great Britain at the Olympics either in 2004, 2008 or 2012. Just Gemma Gibbons, James Austin and Colin would be the eventual Olympians, none of whom had been crowned British champions that day. To any young player who has ever lost to a rival at a young age, never believe your aspirations are at an end – the evidence suggests otherwise, if you battle on.

Although the number three to Stuart Jacob and David Woodcock, Colin was, as a member of the youth squad, still eligible for selection for events where, for the first time, I did not have to subsidise the travel.

The year also saw our first attempts to get Colin ranked in the senior list. At this time, if you finished in the top four of the British rankings, you were seconded to the British senior squad and suddenly your expenses to the monthly squad sessions were covered. On 10 February 2002 at High Wycombe, Colin made his first bid to break through. It proved a disaster as Colin only managed one win, and his brother David placed fifth.

The first tournament in the race to secure selection for the Junior Worlds would be in Bremen, Germany on 24 March 2002. The tournament was one of the toughest in Europe at that time.

Stuart Jacob and Colin secured bronze medals in a massive field of 80 players. Both young men had to win a total of five contests just to secure those bronze medals. It seemed the race would be between the two of them.

In April 2002 Colin took part in his first B Tournament, the British Open (nowadays called a European Cup), and it was a huge entry. The selection of the European Championships at -66k that year was to be made between James Warren or David Sommerville, the two top -66k players at the time to add interest to the day. Not that it concerned Colin – he registered a single win that day at Crystal Palace over a New Zealander Andrew Ross, the last time the British Senior Open was held at that venue (to date, anyway). The win was one of over 200 wins at this international level over a period of 16 years.

Next up would be the Junior A Tournament (nowadays called Junior European Cups) in Russia and a somewhat rude awakening. I had taken Colin across Europe with the club many times and rarely had he returned without a gold medal. In Russia, all Colin could record was one victory; it may have been more had he not tried to readjust a hold down at a crucial moment.

Colin was not selected for the next Junior A in Portugal but neither of his rivals medalled there either. There was the Junior A in France in May and at that time the selection for the Junior Worlds was still in the balance.

Again disaster in France as Colin went out in his first contest, but again neither of his rivals had performed well enough to take a medal so it would now be down to the Venray International in Holland to see who could get their nose in front. The Junior A Tournaments had proved far tougher than I ever expected.

I was less than happy with the set-up in Venray as I was told in no uncertain manner it was bad form for me to coach Colin from the audience and yet other coaches who travelled with the squad, seemed to be doing that all day to their personal players without any complaint.

Maybe it was at this stage I doubted the wisdom of being the father and coach as it made for an almost paranoid combination. Was I being over the top?

The final in Venray was between Colin and David Woodcock. It was a crucial fight as none of the contenders had medalled at the Junior A events. David Woodcock duly won the final. No complaints, but I knew the way back would be very difficult now. In the absence of Junior A medals, the only basis for Worlds selection was likely to be head-to-head confrontations.

The journey home was a quiet one. There was no ray of comfort. Sometimes the best-laid plans could go wrong and they did in just one contest. The lesson learnt in Venray stood me in good stead many years later in the lead-up to London 2012 so far as the danger of head-to-head meetings being measured over past achievements.

We got back on the road very quickly with a senior ranking event the following week when Colin got his first-ever senior ranking points, at the Southern Area Championship. A bronze medal gave him 58-points and suddenly the experience of the Belgian league was beginning to kick in.

There was still a glimmer of hope for selection for the Junior Worlds in Jeju, Korea, and that was an under-20 A Tournament in Poland. However, given the previous form of Colin and his rivals, it was unlikely either would medal and indeed, although Colin won a contest, it was not enough to impress the junior squad manager and with the exit in Poland our hopes faded.

I realised we had no future in the youth squad so turned my attention to the senior rankings and targeted finishing in the top four of Great Britain, which would carry automatic selection for the senior squad. After Poland, we took senior ranking medals in London and Birmingham. The ranking event in London in particular was something of an eye-opener as Colin had been paired in a group with two 2nd Dans. I had many times seen coaches far more experienced than me complain that the draw was wrong and their player should not be in a particular section and even though I noticed at the London event that this appeared to be the case with Colin's first opponent I decided to let it be. My view being you either can or you cannot and on that day the draw was not so important anyway.

We needed a good result at one of the home nation ranking events that carried double points as, by October, Colin was still outside the top four, and the Welsh Senior Open in Cardiff was in my sights.

When we arrived in Cardiff for the Welsh Senior Open, Colin had already been dropped from the next Junior A Tournament, effectively finishing off any chance he might have had of qualifying for selection for the European Junior Championships – that was if there was any real chance of selection. This was at a time when there was this bizarre belief that an athlete has a 'window of opportunity' and if you missed that window you have lost any chance of success. It was actually written somewhere. What a crock! How can you write anyone off because they have missed a target? I was now hearing through the grapevine that Colin had missed his window of opportunity and there was no hope.

All we had left was qualification for the British senior squad. Colin, that day in Cardiff, turned in one of his finest performances, as he battled to reach the final against Gareth Carder, a player who had beaten Colin time after time as cadet players. Gareth was an awesome talent with a wicked stomach throw that was capable of beating anyone in the category. My tactic on this day was to approach Gareth with a very extreme left-handed stance with Colin presenting as little of his full-on body as possible to neutralise the stomach throw. It worked on the day but Gareth was skilful enough to realise that and our future contests would be very different.

In the final on this day Colin edged out Gareth to take the gold in a contest that began the process of turning my hair grey. It was one of many taxing days Gareth had given me over the years as an opponent and all I was doing was sitting in the chair coaching. What Colin and Gareth must have been going through in these hard contests was anyone's guess.

The gold medal must have sent rumblings through the BJA as we then got a call-up to do the Junior A in Germany, I think, but do not know for sure, due to the Dartford Judo Club coach Alan Roberts. We had another chance to steal the European Juniors. Sadly neither Colin nor his rival medalled and David Woodcock secured the double, Junior Worlds and Europeans in the same year based, I think, on that Venray victory. David did not medal and I have to say Colin would not likely have done any better. The draw was so tough for David and would have been for Colin too, but at least David Woodcock had the honour to represent his country at such prestigious events plus a once-in-a-lifetime opportunity to visit Korea.

The end of the year was busy for Colin with a Junior Nationals gold and early exit from the British Senior Nationals and another round of Belgian league meetings, which saw our team reach Division Two. The Welsh Senior Open gold secured a fourth in the British rankings and a spot on the senior team which relieved the disappointment of the youth experience. I was, however, left with the question of what went wrong at the Junior As with Colin. How was it possible that so many excellent European players were out there without my knowledge of them? I had travelled extensively in the Benelux countries and had not come across these players. I still to this day do not know the answer.

Although we finished fourth in the British senior rankings it was very odd that the only medal list that went missing that year was the -66k points from the Heart of England competition where Colin took a bronze. Very strange, but it did not hit Colin's points tally as he had finished in the top four regardless, with or without those points.

In February 2003 we made the long drive to Vise for the Belgium Senior Open. It was our first overseas major international. The day before leaving, Britain and Europe had a deluge of snow but the show had to go on. Looking back, and with the benefit of hindsight, I wonder why we bothered. A nightmare drive across Britain to France and then Belgium in diabolical conditions saw us arrive in Vise at 10.30pm, long after the weigh-in closed. After some friendly persuasion I managed to convince them to let the lads weigh in that night. I had agreed to stay at my friend's place near Antwerp without really looking at the distances involved so a shuttle back and forth to Antwerp followed. By the next morning neither of the players seemed up for the challenge and both my sons lost their opening contests. To be brought back into the competition, the person that beats you must reach the semi-finals, which may not seem too hard until you appreciate the entry in the -66k category was over 80 players. David was lucky enough to get a second fight but the whole trip was a disaster. An awful lot of stress driving and little gained in experience other than that of driving in cruddy conditions in Europe.

This was a time, however, when players fought for experience, not like today when even 13-year-old players only seem to fight if the competition carries ranking points. As such, Colin fought local events at Ipswich and still travelled overseas to low-level competitions in Europe.

Winning the Ipswich Open was actually cited on a television commentary; I think Colin competed at the event even after finishing fifth at the World Championships, quite unusual for a player with such a high profile. It was a great event, sadly lost from the calendar.

In the early part of the year we took a minibus to a tournament just outside Brussels in Belgium. It was not recognised as a major event and did not describe itself as any form of international. We took 12 players into the hall unannounced as the entry instructions were to enrol on the day. I should have guessed by the strange looks we were getting this was not going to be a good day and perhaps we should not be there. Nonetheless, my team got going and the morning turned into a turkey shoot as Kumo's juniors demolished everything in sight. The standard was very low as we rattled off one gold medal after another. By the time we got to the seniors and put Colin on the mat it was already embarrassing and the referee's decisions were getting very questionable to put it mildly, in a bid to slow the demolition of the local judokas. Colin whacked out an easy gold, but David and Robin Smith were now throwing players around the mat, and the officials clearly had a problem seeing them as scoring throws. In a nutshell, it appeared they were trying to save further embarassment by beating some of our seniors. With the benefit of hindsight we should not have been there; the event was not listed as an International and I had brought some very capable players. This was a lower level competition designed for developing local players and probably referees in training so what could I have expected?

At the end of the event the chairman of the club asked my views on the event. Ordinarily I would have just got on the bus and driven home without comment. However, I must have been having a really bad day and as he had asked the question, I told him his referees were not in my view being objective and the event was of a low standard and we had wasted our time coming. It actually took me a little longer to make it that clear and in truth I think I said it more colourfully too. In fact it took me about half an hour to get it all off my chest, so to speak. I was clearly in the wrong and do not feel proud of this incident but there was karma to come.

My rant meant we had to embark on a mad dash to catch the ferry in Calais. A 17-seater minibus is not known for its acceleration and I was never going to put children's lives at risk either so it was not likely we would ever catch that ferry. The tunnel was not an option back then. We missed our booking and the next Sea France ferry was not until four in the morning. P&O were charging a ridiculous amount to board one of their ferries so a night in the ferry car park was ahead of us. With only a vending machine for refreshments, it was a long night listening to the occupants of the bus chatting each other up. Yes, I got exactly what I deserved for my obnoxious behaviour – whilst all the Belgians were tucked up at home drinking Jupiler beer I was stuck all night at Calais with a bunch of kids in an uncomfortable minibus. At the end of the day I owed so much to the Belgians and how they had always looked after us wherever we fought and still now look at the country as my second home.

Driving back the following morning I kept wondering why I had to give my opinion at such length. Would I have expressed my views at such length or with such vigour if I had been aware we would miss the ferry? Probably not. The following year, that Belgian club put on their entry form, 'No overseas clubs allowed.' They may as well just have written 'Kumo Judo Club, stay away' and could I blame them?

The trip to the Northern Irish Senior Open in Belfast saw Colin take gold beating close rival Richard Phillips in the final and a further overseas jaunt to Ede in Holland saw both David and Colin carry off a double gold. The next B Tournament was a long old drive into the fatherland for the German Senior Open. Usually a nation of order and competence, the registration was anything but. Following a long, horrible drive, it took forever to check in; the competition itself was, as you would expect, well run the following day. Colin only managed a single win and David went out first contest. There were many journeys that at the time seemed fruitless and at times it was difficult to motivate myself to plough more money and time into the next venture.

At this time Denise had secured the title of competition controller and we had been running the majority of Eastern Area events for some years. The Eastern Area Closed Championship had fallen apart in the early 90s as the Area's political divide deepened and we had resurrected it in 1999 and, with many club colleagues now table officials, we were capable of running most events, only needing referee support. There had always been a number of Area Committee members that had supported us;

not all had opposed the many changes we had been responsible for. Now, however, we were looking to lift the Area's standing.

The Area Committee had, against mine and Denise's advice, moved the Area base from Thetford to the University of East Anglia in Norwich. This had proved to be a disaster, as competition numbers and grading numbers plummeted. Members of Kumo wound up having to lay and pick up the judo mats following events, sometimes around 300 mats in a day. The only thing in its favour was the size of the arena, which enabled us to run what was, in effect, the very first European Masters Championship. We did write to the European Judo Union and ask if we could call the event the European Veterans Championship; in fact, we wrote three times and never did get a reply. Not to offend the European Judo Union (EJU) or cause any problems for the BJA, we called it the Multi Nations of Europe Masters; it attracted players from over 15 countries including Italy and Austria and was an amazing success.

Soon after, in fact the very next year, the EJU introduced an official version. Of course, the host country would have to pay a rather big sanction fee to the European Judo Union to stage it; little wonder we did not get any response.

This was a minor distraction to the development of Colin, and the rest of the year was spent attending ranking events and lower-level overseas competitions. Colin had seen a level of success with four wins at the British Open (but no medal) and a single win (yes it was that desperate) at the German Open in the July. There was a bronze and gold medal for Colin at the Welsh and Irish Opens respectively, medals that really started to boost confidence and belief, especially the gold from Dublin which had a large international field. In Dublin Vicky put in one of her better overseas performances, taking a silver medal in the youth section. At the British Open Colin's four wins were not as important as his two losses to a couple of French players. I could not work out why Colin had lost until examining the video we had taken. It turned out that both his opponents had been left-handed and Colin really struggled with this even though he too was a leftie. From that point I started to teach all my players to be left-handed as it clearly makes for an awkward fighter.

The Welsh Senior Open was something of a milestone for Colin as he went into the event as the defending champion but lost in the semi-final to Sam Dunkeley. This left Colin with a bronze medal final against World -60k bronze medallist John Buchanan. This contest became more important than the medal itself. I had long admired this player and had followed his career closely. He was a brilliant judoka and, in the words of Colin's long-standing nemesis Gareth Carder, who trained with John Buchanan at Camberley judo club, the hardest-working player you could ever meet. It was the first time I was matside against legendary British team coach Mark Earle, quite a daunting prospect as one from the wilds of Norfolk. Mark Earle was a first-class coach and I have to say I was somewhat in awe of him.

The fight itself was an odd one. At that time it was possible to hold a player on the red mat area for five seconds or so and force a penalty against your opponent or just simply push them out of the fighting area altogether and force a penalty, then go on to win the fight. Indeed, a leading British coach at the time claimed that Great Britain was regarded as the most tactical team at a Junior World Championships simply because they had made winning fights on penalties almost an art form. I would have been far more flattered to be known as the most technical team for variation of throws but each to their opinion and in later years the International Judo Federation brought in rules making it harder to win in this way.

So with this knowledge, the format of the fight with John Buchanan was not a surprise, as our opponent tried to either hold Colin on the red or push him out to get an early penalty score which seemed to be the trend of the time. I knew the likely pattern of the contest. My instruction to Colin was to turn in as John pushed and it worked a treat as my son scored an early 7-pointer in the first exchange with a kind of hip technique. To my mind this was too soon to score as it meant John had some four minutes or so to get the score back and, given John's brilliant standing ability, which was only matched by equally brilliant groundwork, the remainder of the contest was going to be very tight. There were some very tense moments but Colin clung on to a narrow victory and at long last had recorded one of his finest wins.

To this day I treasure this victory, not in any smug way, but because I so admired John's judo, and I have the pleasure of knowing him to this day and my initial belief that he was a first-class gentleman was well founded. Some 12 years later John Buchanan would take a fantastic bronze medal at the Commonwealth Games in Glasgow before finally retiring from a brilliant career with a memorable backflip off the mat. That was a day when I found myself cheering on two Scotsmen, James Millar being the other. Colin would go on to defeat many Olympic and World medallists but this win I treasure, which I hope is the greatest compliment I can pay to this fine athlete.

The end of the year saw Colin take his first National Senior medal, a bronze in a very tough group. It was more memorable given how close some of the early round contests were. We were showing real signs of improvement with two really close defeats against the top two -66kg at the time, David Sommerville and James Warren – the latter actually has the dubious pleasure of holding a victory of a father and son combination – remember I lost to Mr Warren at a grading some years earlier (my son did much better in his fight I hasten to add).

The BJA were quite correctly spending funds on trying to qualify players for the Athens Olympics, and Colin was a long way behind the top two players, David Sommerville and James Warren. Those in the senior squad not considered to be in Olympic contention would very much have to fend for themselves to find their own way forward.

The Belgian league still figured high in our priorities and most of the cost of the travel burden was still with us as a family.

The now annual trip to the Belgium Open was more of a disaster than just the two wins and one defeat and out. Colin returned off the mat after his second win complaining his thumb hurt and I was as usual lacking in sympathy, telling Colin to focus on the next contest against a Japanese player, which he lost.

The next event was a month later, a televised gold medal win at the London International, an event run by a Mr Bernard Richmond, which brought the many judo associations together. I would say the event ran for all too few years as it was a brilliant day and the future site for the judo at the London Olympics. American Bobby Lee took a gold for us; he actually went on to be an elite player fighting for the United States in Continental Opens and was still active in 2016.

Colin was still complaining about his thumb but the show went on and next stop was the New York Open where he lost for bronze against Justin Flores of the USA.

We then crossed the Channel where Colin defeated his brother David in the final to take gold in a massive group in Ieper, Belgium. When we arrived in Ieper we fully expected a group of eight but were presented with an entry of over 30 players. Indeed, Colin fought another three tournaments before we had his thumb looked at. Of course, he had broken his scaphoid and had been fighting for six months effectively with a broken thumb. Strange though it seems, he got some good results, but it really needed fixing and so an operation would put him out for a while. In fact it ended 2004 for him as he was not able to fight again for some six months. It was no real setback as Colin was never in contention for the 2004 Olympics nor did we have any aspirations in that direction.

The rest of the year saw brother David fighting in the Belgian League and I decided to have another crack at the World Masters Championships in Austria having lost for bronze in Ireland in 2002. This was interesting as the last time I visited Austria I was a young hippy type, my hair was long and very dark, not a hint of grey, but I had not come across Gareth Carder at that point who I swear turned me grey. As a 17-year-old, some of the locals treated me like I had the plague, called me an English pig and an ice-cream vendor refused to serve me because she hated the Brits.

I thought during the passage of some 33 years, attitudes would have mellowed. Well, not really; driving through Austria was a nightmare. Austrians may just as well build cars with the horn permanently blowing. Trying to sleep at night was impossible if you opened the window. Even at three in the morning, one impatient clown after another seemed able to find a reason to honk. Also, when they see you walking toward a lift, do they hold the doors? Not a chance. On arrival at the hotel I asked about parking and the receptionist literally threw a card across the counter and walked off.

The tournament saw me win my one and only World medal, on paper. In a group of five I lost all four, but in one fight we put the wrong belts on and came out the wrong side, so I was fighting as this Hungarian guy and he was fighting as Howard Oates. I was all over him throughout the contest but just could not throw him but in golden score I got the penalty and lost, but according to the paperwork I won, and was in the results sheets as winning the bronze. It was actually poetic justice. I only found this out on my return to the UK and saw the printed results and I did write to try and correct the situation, but they never did amend the result. Obviously I have no interest, nor have I ever had any interest, in what we call the 'Wally Bronze' so I would never count the award. Going into 2005 the family had no real belief that we could get anyone in the family to the Olympics. Charlotte and Vicky had dropped away a little from the sport and Colin was struggling to reach the heights necessary to make an impression. My original target for Colin was that elusive 'B' medal (European Cup) but as at 2004 we were nowhere near the level. Brother David moved down a weight to -60 in a bid to improve his fortunes but it looked a hard road for both boys.

THE BID FOR BEIJING 2005–2008

FOLLOWING THE 2004 Olympics, with the retirement of David Sommerville and James Warren (the latter made a brief comeback many years later), the BJA were in position to find a candidate to fill their shoes, so to speak. It would not be easy as there was quite a gap between the country's established number one and two. There were many excellent potential players capable of becoming top-quality players even though many of Colin's rivals had either moved up a weight or had faded from the circuit. The target for us was the newly introduced European Under-23 Championships, to be held for the first time later in 2004. Our main rival, as throughout the cadet and junior journey, was Gareth Carder, but being a year older than Colin he was out of contention in 2005 for the under-23s. His club colleague James Lutman was the most serious threat. There were other good players on the circuit at -66k but they were older than 23 so it precluded them from the European event. Sadly the injury to Colin's wrist prevented him contesting the selection for the very first under-23s which saw Gareth obtain a very commendable seventh place. That is not to say Gareth would not have still got the selection; as I have already said, there was little to choose between the two of them.

The first event Colin was able to compete in, following an operation to repair his thumb, was the Belgium Open in Vise at the end of January 2005. Another long journey to a tournament that was as tough as they get, yet another failure to get among the medals; just two wins and then a loss that resulted in an early journey home. There was another televised London International where Colin took a gold medal and then a Great Britain selection for the Matsumae Cup in Denmark. He travelled with the British squad and took a fifth place. I then paid for both Colin and David to fight in the New York Open in early March 2005. Our friend Pam Lee kindly collected them from the airport and paid for their New York accommodation. Colin's mind was clearly not on the task in hand and he registered just one win before yet another early exit. It was one of Colin's worst overseas performances. Brother David had probably his finest overseas performance in placing seventh in a tough section at -60k.

The BJA selected Colin in late March for his first-ever senior World Cup (nowadays called Continental Opens), in Rome. At this point Colin had been a member of the Great Britain senior squad for over two years, and again managed one win and two defeats and an exit. The following month in Bucharest, Romania returned the same result and although we were picking up wins it really was not enough. It seemed we had not progressed any further than those bad old junior days. The problem for the BJA was that no player at -66k had come near to winning a medal in the weight category since the Sommerville/Warren days. There were many on the circuit all too quick to criticise the BJA for the heavy focus on Warren and Sommerville, seemingly at the cost of the players behind them, but there were few options as these two players were worth investment and were capable of taking medals at the higher level. Perhaps looking back it could be construed a little short-sighted, who knows? There were some fine players who could have bridged the gap between the top two, and those around the level of the younger players like Colin and Gareth, both of whom had shown the potential to progress. Perhaps the BJA had their eyes on an even younger batch of players. Who can tell but it was a second vacuum in the development of Colin, the youth years, when I believed his education was of paramount importance, and the years when the BJA were intent on qualifying their very top players for the Olympics.

The situation simply had to be addressed. We could not depend on the BJA pumping money into Colin; it was still down to the family and our village hall judo club to continue the work. None of us seriously thought the 2008 or any other Olympics were a serious possibility – our results had not supported such an ambition – but we were having fun and enjoying the senior campaign. The cadet and junior circuit was always a strain, mainly due to the conflict you could often find with the parents of your opponents and sometimes the odd coach. On the senior circuit the parents were notably absent and, whilst there were still a number of coaches I found difficult to deal with, I could distance myself from them a little easier. Most of the players were great and the circuit was enjoyable.

We were still fighting Colin and David in the Belgian league and were spending ever-increasing amounts of our time across the Channel but we needed a full-time venue for the brothers to train in. We were fortunate enough to have a somewhat bigger garden than average so I came up with the idea of buying a huge log cabin and matting it out so they could train full-time. Despite viewing many, none fitted my requirements. If we were to do this we would have to build it ourselves, a mammoth task as it would need to take 24 one-metre mats and be high enough to allow throws.

By now we had a number of talented players bordering on senior status, one of whom was Tom Turner, a talented heavyweight. Being close friends with his dad Neil, we set about putting the framework together. Colin, David and I had laid a concrete base. Very much back-breaking work but with the help of a friend's concrete mixer we put down a massive base for the cabin.

Once the skeleton framework was completed with the Turners, the family finished off the structure and we moved 24 one-metre mats into the building to provide a home dojo.

Thomas Turner, better known as just 'Tom', was our heavyweight who won the National Cadet Championship. Alas, he is the only player ever to be mugged on a Kumo tour, much to our amusement. After spending his last fiver on a takeaway burger and fries, two seagulls worked a panzer attack on him at Dover. One swooped in, knocking the burger from his hand, whilst the other whisked it away before it even hit the ground; regretfully no one filmed the event but it is judo folklore at Kumo Judo Club.

It was clear Colin and David needed strength and conditioning help and it just so happened that Jean-Paul Bell, a former player, appeared on the scene and offered to help in this regard in Cambridge, which was very welcome. Every week both brothers would trek down to Dave Southby's fitness centre in Cambridge, whilst training in the cabin and at Kumo Judo Club, where we were now building a serious senior team. At the time I did not realise how serious a role Jean-Paul Bell would play in later years within the British Judo Association.

The cabin years with two brothers fighting each other were somewhat unpleasant. If ever we gave the impression as a family we were completely united, nothing could be further from the truth at times. Some of the wars they had in my back garden could have aroused the interests of the Norfolk Constabulary but somehow it was achieving results. Some years later this cabin would feature on the *One Show* with Chris Evans when Colin made an appearance promoting judo.

We were still fighting in much lower-level events in the Benelux countries and gold or silver medals were now expected. It was clear they had raised their game above club-level tournaments in Europe. But how good were we? At the Romanian World Cup (Continental Open) we recorded one win and claimed a ninth place – it was that desperate, we were grateful for a ninth; I just could not see where a medal at the next level would come from. Colin was now 22 years old, too good for the run-of-the-mill European club tournament circuit, but he still had not won anything of note at a major International.

Colin, David and myself flew to Budapest for the Hungarian training camp. This was before the European Judo Union decided to impose a levy, pushing up the cost of this and other International training camps. It was still not cheap and in David's case something of a disaster. On the very first day he injured his ankle and was unable to train for the whole week. The irony was that he managed to train with the Olympic bronze medallist Jan Kmac, and in the very next randori (spar), against a club brown belt wearing a suit you would expect of a novice, got injured. The lesson being, at a training camp always look for the highest-class player possible; clearly there is less chance of injury. The warm-up was taken by a then little-known kid named Miklos Ungvari who went on to be a fabulous player. Colin had a great week as did I; the food was brilliant. I remember looking at a batch of trays in the canteen with no idea what the food was. The guy in front picked a selection and I just copied him. Fortunately he had very good taste. The only hiccup being the bus driver dropped us off at the wrong terminal which required a mad dash to the correct one to catch our return flight – not made any easier with David's oversized ankle.

There was no obvious choice for the Senior European Championships that year and the BJA gave Colin a lifeline to that event. They offered to pay his cost of travelling to Slovenia (I had no idea where this country was on the map) for a B Tournament (European Cup). Although four British players were travelling, I think only Colin and Gareth Carder were paid for by the BJA. I think James Lutman and Richard Phillips funded themselves. I travelled with Colin as his coach but the BJA did not pay for me; I had to fund myself. The offer was, if we medalled there, we would get selected for the Senior Europeans. Sadly none of the team of -66k players managed to medal, the best performance coming from Richard Phillips who fought great but lost for bronze. Colin won two and lost two; it simply was not good enough.

Again, as one who has sampled booze the world over, I can highly recommend Slovenian beer. We had a very early flight home and our taxi provided by the tournament organisers failed to arrive. The hotel insisted on picking up the tab for the replacement.

We were also treated to a flight home in what was as close as it gets to a private jet. With Gareth Carder, James Lutman, Colin and myself, we were the only passengers on a 28-seat (or so) aircraft, absolute luxury. Just a shame we all bombed out that weekend. On arriving at Gatwick I was unaware there was still a duty-free restriction on cigarettes and I had bought some for my mum who still smoked. A customs officer stopped me and asked how many I had and I was honest and told him how many. He then asked why we went to Slovenia and again I told him and was honest and said we did not get any medals. He took another look in my bag, stared again at the amount I had and told us our weekend seemed bad enough as it was and to clear off. My mum was very grateful to him.

In June that year we paid for a trip to Italy for the Tre Torri International. Attached to the event was a training camp the following week. This was another training camp not subject to European Judo Union levies and was relatively cheap. With the EJU taking over more and more camps over the coming years their cost was increasing as host countries would have to pay a European Judo Union to run them. I very much agree with the many great changes brought about by the European Judo Union but on this aspect I think it made such camps inaccessible to the poorer player. This being said, the European Judo Union does help those with promise.

It was, I thought, the last training camp I would have to pay for but, as it turned out, I would help pay for Colin's very last one many years later. The whole trip was a disaster. Colin and David made early exits from the competition and although there were Japanese and Russian teams there, it seemed they did not attend the days we did and, when they did, trying to train with them was difficult. It appeared they had their sights set on the named players and Colin and David, not exactly big names on the international scene, were not worthy opponents. It was also odd that on the day the drugs testers turned up, a number of those high-profile players were conspicuous by their absence, something I pointed out to the organiser who had not previously noticed.

The week was very boring, the locals were not too friendly either. We managed to find a bar (yes, I always manage that) run by a Slovenian lady who looked after us and translated what the food was. We also made friends with a very green lizard and even took photographs of him. Other than that, the only memorable part about that trip was the flight there and back over the Alps.

There was still no natural selection at -66k for the World Championships in Egypt in September and I did not think we had any chance in view of our results. There was a new B Tournament in Istanbul in July. It came with an offer that I think very few people noticed. The organiser would provide free accommodation for participants in a hotel. It looked a good deal so I entered both Colin and David, and booked the flights.

The week we were due to fly out to Turkey saw the announcement that London had won the right to host the 2012 Olympic Games. I remember feeling somewhat emotional at the announcement. So many had worked so hard, it was just reward for their efforts. I certainly did not think we would ever be a part of it.

Sadly, the Wednesday before our Friday departure saw the 7/7 London bombings; it was the day after London had been announced as the host of the 2012 Olympics. I recall reading 'Pourquoi Londres?' (Why London?) on a French newspaper at the airport. I thought this related to our capital being bombed; not so, it was why London and not Paris as the site of 2012. I still like to think it was an early edition.

I gave long and hard thought before leaving for Heathrow as to whether any sport was worth the risks involved in making this journey at such a sensitive time. On reflection it was probably the safest time ever to travel.

Flying into Istanbul we did not know what to expect. We had travelled through a lightning storm and experienced a somewhat rocky flight. As you approach Istanbul airport there are many mosques that stand out against the coastline.

Neither of us had ever experienced a Middle Eastern country and I was a little apprehensive to say the least. I need not have been as our welcome was superb. The hotel was great and the pick-up from the airport went very smoothly. Being used to the regimented process of registering at the German Open in particular, I asked an official when registration occurred. There was clearly something lost in the interpretation as he thought we had not entered. This was still not a problem; he helpfully and hastily started preparing cards, until I realised there was no registration. It was that laid-back an event; the Turkish people were brilliant.

I had long lowered my sights for Colin to that of just winning a B Tournament medal (nowadays referred to as a Senior European Cup); on his previous form that was the best I thought we would get. With regard to David, I thought let us just enjoy the ride and pick up the odd international medal below that of B Tournaments; anything else would be a bonus.

The day of the event saw David very unlucky not to progress at -60k where, not for the first or last time, he would be robbed of a victory that would almost certainly have put him among the medals. Colin got off to a fine start with two wins and faced an Israeli player in the quarter-finals. Without being too disrespectful, it looked a formality, as the Israeli player did not look very strong. However, Colin again dropped to a terrible defeat and what followed was a blazing row between the two of us. I had become sick of paying out for these trips only to see a player not fully focused on the task. I made it clear to Colin this was the last trip I would pay for and it seemed to do the trick as he won his repechage contest to set up a bronze medal fight with Zaza Kedelashvili from Georgia.

This would be the first time Colin had contested for a medal at this level and would fulfil my expectation of what he could realistically achieve at the sport. The fight was a titanic battle with a player who just six months later would be crowned European champion. From behind, Colin came back to win his first-ever medal at elite level. David, who was holding the video camera, was shaking so much he missed the winning throw. Colin's superior fitness was eventually the difference between them.

That night we celebrated in the hotel with beer and wine. I thought we may well have also secured a shot at the Worlds in September as this was one of the highest medals won by a -66k player since the retirement of James Warren and David Sommerville. I would say our old rival Gareth Carder had turned in a fantastic performance at the German open a year earlier taking a silver medal.

We returned home the following day and accordingly informed the BJA. It must be remembered that results were still not freely posted or available on the internet. The suggestion was the event was weak (even though Miklos Ungvari, the future London 2012 silver medallist, went out in an early round; to be fair he sustained a head injury and withdrew otherwise the results would have been very different).

The BJA, however, announced that they would run trials inviting the top ten -66k players. A nightmare date was looming with the winner being considered for the -66k spot in Egypt.

There was a certain irony here in that I was the champion of the trials in the Eastern Area and now found myself in this scenario to select a player for the World Championships via trials and not too keen on the prospect. I thought we had done enough to gain automatic selection.

On the day of the trials our nerves were at breaking point. All the players' names were put into a hat and two pools were created. Given that the top ten -66k players were there, each pool was equally horrendous.

There was, however, one noticeable withdrawal on the day, that being Jean-Rene Badrick, a brilliant 16-year-old junior who had been winning national and international medals in the youth section. His absence was a relief to me as I had watched him for the past couple of years and was well aware of the threat he posed.

The pool Colin drew meant a first fight against Gareth Carder. It must have been their 16th or so encounter over the years and neither player had anything in their armoury the other did not know. The fight was tense with Gareth drawing first blood with a yuko (5-point score) and frankly I thought that would be it. However, with just seconds on the clock, Colin scored a waza-ari (7-point score) and won the contest. It would be such a bitter pill for Gareth who would not lose another contest that day, which would mean he lost a crack at the World Championships by just a few seconds. Colin and James Millar also met yet again that day.

Colin battled through to the final pool where he won both his contests, the last of which was a gruelling war with Alex

Farbon. I remember Mark Earle walking up to me and offering his hand as at that point the penny still had not dropped it was over. The first major selection for Colin would be the Senior World Championships in Cairo and what an ironic twist. Not so much a selection but a spot based on what occurred on the judo mat. The very reason I had built up an army of enemies in the Eastern Area, my love of the trials system. The non-selection for the European Cadets, Youth Olympics, the Junior European and Worlds suddenly seemed totally lacking in importance. Nobody could argue with this one. We won this selection. I did not doubt for a moment that Colin stood little chance in Cairo but we were getting an opportunity. In the past there had been many others that stood little chance but they still got selected so we thought justice had finally been done.

That evening I attended a friend's birthday party where, not for the first time I hasten to add, I made a bit of an ass of myself. Many tell me it was the mixing of vast quantities of red and white wine that was the culprit. I would forever joke that someone spiked my drink rather than admit I had overdone the wine. In the final analysis, it probably was not important what caused my memory blank from 7.30 onward that evening but it did mean I had licence to act (and apparently did) like a total plonker. I have many times consumed a little more than the recommended weekly intake of wine but never had, before this occasion, a total blank of the previous evening. Such was the pressure of the morning I think my body was in some type of meltdown.

Amazingly British Judo agreed to pay for my flight to Cairo which was a magnificent gesture. Although I would not be an official coach or in Colin's matside chair I felt somewhat honoured. Maybe I could gain some recognition as a coach after all.

As an 18th birthday present to my daughter Vicky, I treated her to the weekend (well, the word on the street was I was rich) in Cairo to see Colin although in reality she came for the museum and the pyramids. We flew out of Norwich to Schipol and were to catch a connecting flight to Cairo. The flight to Holland was delayed and although Vicky and I were fast enough to catch the connecting flight to Egypt evidently our baggage was not, as we found on arrival at our destination. Stepping out of the aircraft in the early hours of the morning was an unbelievable experience as the night heat nearly knocked you off your feet.

It did not take us long to work out our baggage was not there so we took our pre-booked taxi to the hotel. The room was awesome as you would expect, and the staff really helpful, giving us toothbrushes to make up for the mislaid baggage which arrived the following day.

The day Colin fought was not that memorable. A first round bye saw Colin up against Milos Mijalkovic, a contest you might have expected him to win. Alas, despite a penalty lead, throughout the fight Colin lost on a 7-point score toward the end and was eliminated from the competition. Oddly enough I was more fascinated by my environment than Colin competing. The arena had every front row seat occupied by what appeared to be college students who did not seem to be interested in the proceedings. The arena was otherwise very sparse. On seeing a video of the Worlds on TV some months later I realised why that was. On television, with all the front row seats occupied, it gave the impression the arena was full. Clearly it was a rent-a-crowd situation. Indeed, a number of young men in the crowd would sit by the side of me throughout the day and make conversation. Their real intentions were to talk to my daughter Vicky; the blonde is a rarity in Egypt.

Anyhow, back at the hotel, Vicky and I were about to learn more cultural lessons. With the hotel, I booked an organised tour of the museum and the pyramids.

I expected a 30-seater coach and tour guide for my Egyptian pounds. Imagine my shock when outside the hotel there was an MPV and a tour guide and we were the only occupants of his van. We reluctantly got in and drove off (we would never do that nowadays). In fact, he drove along a four-lane highway; there were actually only three lanes marked on the road but this did not seem an issue with our driver or anyone else on the road – nor did the potholes in the road or the lack of concern for other drivers, which perhaps explained the numerous dents on just about every vehicle we passed. As to the road workers! Health and safety did not seem to exist as these unfortunate workers had cars whizzing centimetres past their backsides at 70mph. A pick-up truck went past us loaded with about 20 people standing and desperately hanging on to anything they could in the back. At times I doubted we would get to the museum in one piece but of course that was not our first stop.

As part of the tour we stopped at some premises where we were going to be shown how the Egyptians made paper.

Apparently they were the first culture to make the stuff. In all honestly I did not care who makes it now or 10,000 years ago; so long as it fits in my photocopier, I am happy, but we went through the motions and listened, pretending to be interested. Of course then we are shown paintings on this paper which we were clearly expected to buy. I agreed to buy one and the salesperson tried a hard sale on a second until I threatened not to buy the first one. In fairness it was not expensive but I did not want it; such is life, if it got us out and to the museum, which was the place I booked, so be it.

The tour of the museum was amazing and following that we were taken to the pyramids which are not in the middle of the desert but on the edge of town. I was pleased to learn it was the French who shot the nose of the Sphinx and not the Brits. The only blight there being a bunch of youths shouting at us, one of whom seemed to be stating I was English but apparently did not have a father. This caused great embarrassment to our guide but he still had one more surprise visit. A perfume shop! Really, did either of us bargain for this? The nightmare continued, another hard sell and there was no way out without making a purchase. Fortunately we got Colin to pay later for the perfume as a present for his girlfriend. In reality the tour was an organised mugging.

We had dinner with Colin that evening before preparing to fly back in the early hours of the morning. At about two in the morning I asked reception at the hotel to call for a taxi. The man at reception told me in an irate manner there was no way that he would ring for a taxi for me. He said it would be too dangerous that time of night and instead he would arrange for the hotel limo. I thought it was another ruse to get money out of me until he said compliments of the hotel and he wanted to make sure we got to the airport safely.

He was true to his word but my night was not over yet. All I wanted to do was get home.

After checking in, the passport control officer dropped my boarding pass under a machine. In my temper I turned and walked straight into a glass door and made myself look a complete idiot in the process much to my daughter's amusement and everyone else watching. It was one of those nights and the sooner we got on the plane the better.

The flight home went without further incident and we got safely back to Norwich.

There was still one more major event, that being the European Under-23s in Kiev in November. With Gareth slightly older than Colin it meant the main rival would be James Lutman. In their meetings at junior level Colin had the edge, but James was a wonderful judo player, exciting to watch and had an abundance of techniques. If James had any faults it was his inability to take a step backwards. No matter how far ahead James could be in a contest he would always look for the knockout score, an attribute lacking in so many players, and it meant James was always a dangerous opponent. In the Welsh Senior Open final we faced James for what turned out to be the last meeting between the two players and Colin ran out a narrow winner in a tight contest. The win secured the Under-23s in Kiev. The next time I ran into James was at the Commonwealth Tournament in Walsall in 2019 where he took a gold medal in the Masters section; he was still a brilliant player.

Colin's next tournament would be in Genk, Belgium, the following month. We originally thought the tournament was in Ghent which is, of course, nowhere near Genk, but you have to admit they look like nearly the same place. So we had to unbook the hotel in Ghent and rebook one in Genk. This may seem like a daft mistake but Belgium is a country with four official languages. As such you can set off from western Belgium driving to Luik when halfway along the journey its name changes to Liege. It can be confusing.

Anyhow, the tournament in Genk was pretty much a waste of time; Colin and David won golds in a canter and clearly we had passed this level of tournament or Colin would have to move up a weight to make them harder. At this event we learnt a little about concussion. One of our players, Aaron Pearce, took a knock in his first fight but we thought nothing of it and sent him out for his second. To my horror he looked like a rag being blown in the wind and, when he lost quite quickly and came back to the matside bench, he kept asking David when his first fight was due. We immediately took him to the doctor who diagnosed the condition and we pulled him out. He recovered okay and still remains a Kumo player.

The following month I took David to the Irish Senior Open in Dublin where he took gold in quite an international field. Given David was Colin's main training partner this was all to the good as David had reached a good standard by now and, with the back garden cabin training, things were progressing nicely.

In October a trip to the Swedish Open in Boras saw Colin and David both make early exits but in reality our minds were on the Under-23 Europeans in Kiev. We met with a margin of success as one of our lady players, Emma Paflin, placed fifth at the event, which demonstrated the depth of skill developing at a rural village hall in the middle of nowhere. Emma would stay with us for many years to come, and still remains a close friend today. The Swedish Open was held in a place called Boras and, as was the tradition on a Kumo trip, we would stock up on the booze on the Sunday but, to our horror, found all the off licences were closed. We did manage to buy low-alcohol beer – what a waste of money that was, a little like buying a car without wheels. Even the dinner they put on left you looking for a fish and chip shop. Of course, the Eastern European teams, of whom there were many, seemed to think they were in heaven but most of the Benelux teams and the Brits were less than happy.

Next up was the European Under-23 in Kiev, Ukraine.

I flew out of Norwich to Kiev whilst Colin travelled with the British squad from London. I had the task of driving Colin to Heathrow, returning home and then getting Denise to drive me up to Norwich for my flight on the same day.

On this occasion I had to meet the full cost of travel. Despite my GCE O level in Geography in truth I had no idea where Ukraine was. I knew the Beatles wrote a song about the place but I doubt whether even John Lennon had ever been there.

The flight was long and lonely. Travelling solo is quite hard especially during long waits for connecting flights. Back in 2005 all your mobile phone did was make phone calls; there were no games or other distractions on them.

Eventually I landed in Kiev and received a pop star welcome – or so I thought. As I walked through into the arrivals from the main airport, I was surrounded by hordes of men shouting and screaming at me. Unfortunately the language bears no resemblance to anything I have ever encountered before – I can just get by in France, Holland, Belgium and Germany, but here there was no chance of understanding their alphabet.

As I bundled through the crowd I suddenly realised they were all taxi drivers trying to get my fare. I beckoned to them toward a man holding a piece of cardboard with 'Oates' written on it and then had an angry reaction of abuse from those in the horde. They were clearly angry I had pre-booked a taxi, but many seemed to have suddenly picked up the English language; in fairness, some of the words I heard had a somewhat universal meaning, mostly beginning with 'F'.

Once on board the drive to the hotel was like something from a James Bond movie. There were Ladas everywhere (yes, Ladas, those cars modelled on a 1930s Russian tank now banned in Europe) and huge bulky trucks spewing out black soot from their exhausts. Maybe there was a language barrier between the taxi driver and me but it seemed he had the personality of a plank of wood; however, we got to the hotel safely.

I stayed at the tournament hotel which was as expected – very plush. Colin and I met up briefly but he was with the squad and he returned to his room to prepare for the morning weigh-in. I had something of a disturbed night as the ceilings seemed excessively thin and I was kept awake for long periods by the downstairs occupants; I sincerely hope to this day they were not members of the British squad. It seemed they would never run out of energy. Whichever country they were fighting for there was no chance of a medal from either of them but I had nothing but admiration for both athletes' stamina and endurance; their coaches would have been immensely proud of them.

There was never a possibility I would be matside with Colin at an event like this but somehow I got into the warm-up area that morning. What an eye-opener that was. I was surrounded by a bunch of lads whose ages were all supposed to be under 23. There was one player who took his jacket off revealing not what I would describe as a hairy chest and back but more like fur; yes, I had discovered a human being who looked more like a yeti than a man. This particular guy was meant to be just 20, yet housed an environment on his back that might still have been home to a colony of mammoths. There were 19-year-olds with five o'clock shadows at midday. In a nutshell there were some ringers in there without doubt. Some years later I would have to listen to a senior voice in the BJA stating our players must start to perform at younger ages. Clearly some of these people do not get out much or turn a blind eye.

On the mat Colin lost his opener against a Greek lad, Revazi Zintiridis, and then won a fight at this level for the first time ever, against Dragan Crnov. In the repechage, Colin was beaten by Zaza Kedelashvili, a player he had earlier beaten in Turkey.

During the tournament Colin needed to change his trousers and made the mistake of doing it in front of where I was sitting, apparently a serious offence of breaching a restricted area. This aroused the wrath of a very obese and even more obnoxious Ukrainian official who came over shouting and threatening to expel Colin from the event. Clearly this was a man used to getting his own way especially, at the dinner table. All that was necessary was the reasonable approach, no need for bullying tactics. So far, my experience of dealing with Ukrainian men had not been a pleasant one.

Colin may well have been eliminated but Ian Feenan was fighting for a bronze medal at -73k. I knew Ian through his dad Jim, who had beaten me a couple of time on the Masters circuit. If my trip had been unpleasant, what followed for Ian was disgraceful. Halfway through the fight he threw his Russian opponent for a winning score. Not for the first time, there were the usual remonstrations from the Russian contingent and the score was waived off and Ian eventually lost. Trying to beat a Russian in Ukraine was never going to be easy if at all possible and it was heartbreak for Ian.

Colin and I spent the evening at TGI Fridays in Kiev. Walking the streets of Kiev was an odd feeling as it did not feel like a European country. The men in uniform cluttered around the streets seemed more menacing than reassuring.

The meal at TGIs was up to its usual standard and went down nicely with my wine.

I could drink even if Colin could not. I began to realise what the Beatles meant in the *White Album* song 'Back in the USSR' and the lines 'the Ukraine girls really knock me out they leave the West behind'. Well it is doubtful the Beatles had ever been to Kiev at this point but how right they were. Most of the women I had met there were stunning regardless of their age and they were so friendly. They certainly made up for their counterpart men. Again the men were all built like Mr Universe (well, apart from the obese guy at the tournament) but I had found them so miserable, unhappy and quite rude. I found the concept of positioning a big burly guy outside what seemed to be every shop with the power to search shoppers leaving the store amazing. It was a sure fact you did not argue with these guys either.

The following day I said goodbye to Colin and the next time I would see him would be when I picked him up from Heathrow on his return flight. At Kiev airport there was just one more twist in the tale. As I stood in the duty-free shop I could not help but notice a rather attractive, I assumed Ukrainian, lady staring at me. I thought, my word, I have cracked it at my age. I had pulled in Ukraine. Bearing in mind my admiration of Ukrainian ladies in general I was on cloud nine. Alas she approached me and asked if I had any Ukrainian currency on me (at that time you were not allowed to leave the country with Ukrainian notes). She flashed some card at me; I assume she was customs, although with an alphabet that bears more resemblance to my youngest grandson's scribble than to ours it could have been a milk monitor's card. I explained all I had was dollars and she walked off. I am not too sure if I was disappointed or not. There must have been many more situations on the planet more unpleasant than being arrested and interrogated by her.

As Colin was still living in North Lopham with us, I had to juggle my travel arrangements around his far more than

I would have liked. I was still working in a filthy chicken factory and it was hard graft to always be there for Colin when required.

The year had been a success only in the fact that Colin was now in the selection process. Although Colin had won events like the Irish and Welsh Opens, we still needed an international title with some weight. The British Senior Open was historically a massive event but, with various venue and date changes, the numbers had dwindled somewhat. When this event was held at Crystal Palace it would often attract over 400 players but now it was down to around 250 or so.

The event was being held at Burgess Hill and was still regarded as an event worth winning. The -66k was not massive with around 20 or so players; the only non-Brit Colin would fight if he reached the final was the American Taylor Takata, quite a useful performer. However, Colin did reach the final, recording four victories en route, and his opponent would be Gareth Carder yet again. The form book proved correct and the enemies of old were once again pitted against each other in the final of the British Senior Open.

At this stage Colin had really won very little at any international level and, although this was not as heavily subscribed as the many before, I desperately wanted Colin to win this one.

Before Colin walked out to face Gareth in the final I remember saying to him, in far more graphic language, 'Do not mess this up, you may never get another chance to win an Open.' Colin will tell another version of the language used, similar to the words the Ukrainian taxi drivers were using, but those words are not for print.

The contest was the usual grind with both lads giving their all. Gareth had turned my hair grey since his junior days and in his senior career had done an equally good job on my beard. It seemed Gareth Carder was responsible for single-handedly turning me into a Santa Claus lookalike; on a brighter note it could be said I could always find seasonal work, thanks to him.

Colin ran out a close winner and took his first major gold but such events were not point-scoring for the Olympics in China, which still seemed a long way away.

We ended 2005 and the future looked rosy; we managed to emerge as number one in Britain but there was one notable absence at the British Open and that was the super junior Jean-Rene Badrick. I still had a very vigilant eye on this young man who it seemed was turning over all in his path. This young superstar had already won a European Cadet Championship beating the brilliant Frenchman Ugo Legrand, who went on to medal at the London Olympicsalong the way. Nonetheless, it seemed the 2006 Senior Europeans in Finland would be ours.

In 2006 there were two targets: the Europeans in Finland and the Commonwealth Tournament in Ireland. We felt we had the Europeans pretty well sewn up but the Commonwealths were later in the year and we expected a strong challenge for that spot from the English judoka.

The Great Britain squad had not been centralised at this stage. There was a centre at Bisham Abbey but for the most part the GB team would meet for weekend sessions every month or so. In essence the top players still trained at their clubs, which allowed the personal coaches a high input. Indeed, much higher than today.

I continued to enter Colin for more tournaments in Belgium but now moved him up to -73k to make life harder. This had the desired effect as now Colin was losing the odd contest, such as in Nivelles where he only took silver. Another trip to the Belgium Senior Open produced a couple of wins but no medals. Our attention was mainly focused on Colin's selection for the Super A Tournament in Paris (now called a Grand Slam). In truth Colin was not ready for this one, but fighting at this magnificent event was an opportunity too good to refuse and often could prejudice any future selection.

Denise and I travelled to Paris just to watch one contest and see our son make an early exit if only we could have actually seen the fight. In fact, from where we were sitting, you needed binoculars to see the closest fight and our son was of course on the farthest mat in the arena – our main memory being the atmosphere in the arena and watching our son come out to fight, with some 15,000 people watching. Even if Colin was never to make the grade it was still a memorable occasion. The experience I learnt was never to drive in Paris again; it was a nightmare. The emergence of Eurostar was most welcome and a much better way of travelling.

Next up was the Dutch World Cup (Continental Open) and another long drive up to Rotterdam and one win and an exit. At this event I started to become somewhat agitated as Colin was sent out to fight Alim Gadonov with the instruction to blitz him in the first minute, contrary to my advice which was to take his time. At this stage, even with my limited knowledge of the international circuit, I knew Russians were at their most deadly early in a contest and, given Gadonov was an astonishing fighter anyway, I could not believe the advice coming from his camp. I now firmly believed the player's personal coach should always have been in the matside chair. In fairness, without any centralised system, how did the GB coaches know how to matside coach a perfect stranger? The only time they saw a player was at an elite competition. Anyhow, Colin was clearly beaten. The only lasting memory of this trip was a little Italian restaurant we found in a Rotterdam back street.

We continued fighting Colin in the Belgian league where he now went up and down the weights, which continued to help his development.

In April Colin was selected for the World Cup in Portugal and at last the breakthrough, well almost. It may be hard to imagine but there were no live results online at that time so we had to wait for Colin to call. We got to a state where the longer it took to ring us we thought it meant the further he got. Sometimes that just was not true; we would wait seemingly forever only to be told it was a late fight and that he was out. On this occasion he rang and told us he was fighting for bronze against Javier Delgado. It was not a fight I expected Colin to win and eventually we got the call informing us of a fifth place. Not quite the breakthrough medal but four wins at this level (in today's Continental Opens) are more than enough wins to register a medal.

There would be one more trip to the Belgian league, in April, before Colin would jet off to Tampere, Finland and his first crack at the Senior European Championships. The journey to Finland went without incident once I appreciated the place never gets dark in summer. Again Colin travelled with the British squad but I travelled alone and on arrival went to get a burger in town at 10.30 in the evening, still in daylight, before settling down in my hotel. The town of Tampere is quite beautiful and friendly as are all the Nordic countries.

The competition site was a fair way from me so I took a taxi there. Colin had an okay draw against Hovhannes Davtyan but again not a sparkling performance and, not for the first time at a major event, was eliminated. The interesting aspect of the day was the performance of Zaza Kedelashvili who Colin had beaten in Turkey but had lost to in Kiev, who took the first of his three gold European Championships. At this stage I started to think the gap was not so great after all.

I managed to bunk a ride on the tournament bus back to the team hotel where Peter Cousin (Peter would take a European bronze that weekend and then go on to take a fantatstic World silver in Rio the following year) kindly offered me his lunch ticket. In fairness he did say the food was not good but I was starving hungry and was grateful for the gesture. I do not think I ever told Peter how right he was about the food. I had a long walk home that evening to my hotel but with the eternal sunlight it seemed a good idea and I could also pick up a burger to get rid of the taste of the team hotel food.

On returning to England I bounced Colin straight back across the Channel, this time to Holland where he ripped off six wins and another gold at -73k.

Next up would be the Commonwealth Tournament in Derry, Northern Ireland. I had already sampled the tournament site as I had lost for bronze when the World Masters was held there. The atmosphere there was a little tense in 2002, it not being too long after what is described today as 'The Troubles'. By 2006, following the Good Friday Agreement in 1998, it was a little less tense and the tournament was a great success, with Colin taking another (so far as I was concerned) good standard international gold. Colin's main rival was James Millar, a brilliant -60k player who had moved up a weight. They met in the semi-final with Colin victorious and then he beat Lee Calder of New Zealand in the final. Many years later Colin and James would again meet in the Commonwealth Games. Although I again could not officially coach, Alan Roberts, the England manager, told me to just shout over the top if I wanted to, which I did, and against James it was very necessary as that was a close one. The South African party stood out as a great bunch of characters, chanting and singing throughout the day.

At this stage we had crossed the Irish Sea on countless occasions and, to break up the monotony, I always picked a different way to get there. For this trip it was a Ryanair flight into Dublin and a hire car to take us up to the north of Ireland. What harm could there being doing that, you may wonder? Well, driving into a supermarket in Derry, I was constantly hooted by other cars. So when I parked up, thinking as you do that there was a fault with the car, I checked it over for problems before driving back out after shopping. To my amazement I received a barrage of hooting again but this time ignored it. On returning to Norfolk I mentioned it in passing to an Irish friend who asked the question, where did I hire the car? I explained in Dublin, to which he said having Catholic number plates in a Protestant part of Derry was the probable cause of the hooting barrage. Who would have thought that?

Sometime after the trip to Ireland, a member of the BJA's employees arranged to visit me in Norfolk to ascertain training requirements for Colin. At last I thought someone will listen to the problems we have. The individual sat with their clipboard and pen, as they do, making meticulous notes. I told this person we needed Eastern Bloc training camps and tournaments in Russia. We drank some tea, ate some digestives and said goodbye. A month or so later two other -66k players, Richard Phillips and Gareth Carder, were selected for a trip to Russia to compete in a tournament and training camp.

I could not believe someone could just waste their time and mine. Unfortunately neither of the players got to Russia as all aircraft were grounded on the day of departure following revelation of the liquid bomb plot, and I remember being told the traffic in and around the airport was gridlocked, so I actually dodged a bullet with Colin's non-selection.

Beyond the Commonwealths there was yet another trip to Belgium and a bronze at -73k, and a gold at -73k in the Irish Senior Open after beating the excellent Irishman Gerard Turner in a televised final. With cameras recording the two finalists being led to the mat by young girl judo players, Colin waited patiently for the announcement of the names and, as Gerard walked on to the mat, Colin ran off and pushed the little girl to face his opponent instead. The little girl found it highly amusing even if the organisers did not see the funny side. The fight was a cracker with Colin just hanging on to a slim lead. Had the fight gone another minute I am not sure Colin could have clung on to win as Gerard was such a strong and skilful fighter.

All was going to plan, but I still had a close eye on Jean-Rene Badrick as he was so young I was rather hoping he might have a growth spurt and turn into a -73k player, and there was also our old buddy Gareth Carder still knocking on the door. I approached the British Senior Closed with Colin knowing we had everything to lose and not very much to gain. There was one more trip to prepare Colin for the British and that was a six-win gold medal at -73k in Rouen, France where the organisers were kind enough to pay for our accommodation; his brother David turned in a brilliant display but lost for bronze after registering four fine wins.

At the British Trials, or Senior Closed as it is also called, the format for entering and the method of competition was often changed and this event was no different. There was a knockout system at this one and I could see instantly that we would have Gareth Carder in the semi-final if the fights went to form. Jean-Rene Badrick was on the other side of the draw with what I thought, even at his youthful age, was a clear run to the final. In these situations you often hope your main rivals will clash and I would have preferred Gareth to have clashed with Jean-Rene before meeting Colin. It would have made the day easier.

The form book prevailed and Colin faced Gareth for a place in the final. As usual the two rivals fought out a tight match. During the fight Colin was down on penalties and it has always been our philosophy to go for broke if we are losing and so I waved Colin in and Gareth did the business and caught him with a winner. There would be no match with Jean-Rene Badrick for us. Colin went on to take bronze but our position was now weakened. Not for the first time, Colin and I exchanged some pleasantries, and he was further outraged by me telling him today was JR's day and, had they fought, JR would have won. To this day he disagrees. JR went on to come from behind and beat Gareth and claim the British crown. Before this event the BJA had announced that the criteria for selection for the 2007 Europeans would be based on the British Closed, the Belgium Open and the British Open. One would have thought losing at the British might not have been so bad but Colin had never come close to a medal in Belgium and that would leave heaps of pressure on the British Open. I realised we were in trouble. I knew the BJA were looking for a new prospect and I have to admit I thought they had found him and it was all but over for us. This being said, I also remember thinking that, even if Colin had beaten Gareth that day, I did not think we would have beaten Jean-Rene Badrick and, had Colin lost, there would have been no way back whatsoever. My gut feeling was that our time to take on this brilliant young player had not yet arrived.

The British Senior Open was first up and Colin had an awful draw, while on the other side, Jean-Rene Badrick's draw looked quite comfortable. Colin made a third-round exit while Badrick took silver.

At the Belgium Senior Open Jean-Rene Badrick bowed out early as Colin lost for bronze but, even though I knew a fifth in Belgium was better than winning the British Closed, it was clear it would not impress the BJA in lieu of Badrick's British Senior Open silver.

As far as the Europeans was concerned we were out of the running. With a rival so young and talented I did wonder whether there was any way back.

Colin could have embarrassed the selectors by performing at the Polish World Cup but both he and Jean-Rene made first-round exits there. Badrick went off to the Europeans where he lost his first fight to Oscar Penas. A very hard opener for any player and I am not so sure Colin would have fared any better.

For Colin though it was back to basics. The cabin work was going well, the strength and conditioning with Jean-Paul Bell was in full flow and training partners at Kumo were in abundance, particularly brother David.

There were more trips to Belgium in the shape of the Belgian league and overseas training with our sister club Kemzeke in Stekene. A gold in Lommel again at -73k (during which I heard a Belgium coach describe Colin as crazy as he ripped through his opponents), which by now had become our overseas fighting weight, and a bronze at the Swiss Open in beautiful Lausanne followed, a trip funded by the Eastern Area who by now had started to help fund many of our trips overseas.

Under the chairmanship of David Etchells-Butler, the Area Committee was helping to develop senior judo in the East. The event on paper was a mild success as Colin took bronze but yet again it did not paint the true picture as, in his semi-final, Colin was trailing by a small score against a Russian player when he produced a fabulous winning throw in the dying seconds. The big screen showed the move maybe three times before the Russian contingent made a considerable noise, ranting and raving, and suddenly the clearly winning throw was removed from the big screen as the referees had a discussion before disallowing the throw. It was a disgusting show of giving in to aggression. The Russian coach later that day saw me in a supermarket and gave me a big hug and apologised for the decision he had fought to reverse. The day had been worse for David in the repechage final when he threw his Austrian opponent for a winning throw. The referee was in no doubt it was David's throw but the two line judges overruled him and gave the throw to the Austrian player. Both the line judges were of course Austrian. However, if you want to win, the only way is to put the result beyond any doubt and you do that by being head and shoulders above your opponent.

When I booked the trip I arranged the flight home for a Monday without realising Colin, David and Emma were fighting on the Saturday, leaving Sunday free. We toured Lausanne in brilliant sunshine with temperatures at 21°C yet surrounded by snow-covered mountains with a beautiful lake by the side of the town. Eventually we found a bar showing the Chelsea v Man Utd Premier League match. Drinking European lager in such conditions does not get much closer to paradise; it made up for the day before and it has to be mentioned, as far as Emma's contests were concerned, we thought she had a straightforward opener with an Australian girl who turned out to be Russian, so another defeat. Somehow the judo was not the highlight of that weekend.

However, the Great Britain performances were still not good enough; a seventh at the World Cup in Italy was followed by a first-round exit in Romania. At the same time there were no successes for any -66k player at these events and we hoped that Colin's gold medal at the Northern Irish Senior Open would tip the scales back in our favour and win selection for the World Championships in Rio. Despite the fact that no senior player had performed, we received the news of Jean-Rene Badrick's selection for the Worlds just after Colin took gold in Belfast. It was a real downer. We had chased our rivals all year but whenever we fought, somehow, some way, they did not seem to be there. The lessons learnt here stood us in good stead in the lead up to the London Games, the moral of the story being, once your nose is in front do not give anyone any chance to catch your tail.

I think it was due to the seventh in Italy that people started asking me to appeal the decision on the World selection but I had no intention of doing that. Indeed Mr Badrick's coach Leigh Davies even asked me why I had not appealed and I simply told him that I believed there were 20 players out in Rio that could beat Colin and I was not going to put that type of pressure on him or make him look a fool. Also I had matured as a coach and now realised that a coach and player make their own luck and subsequent selections by getting results; my days of blaming referees or officials or anyone else, the BJA included, were becoming a thing of the past.

Whilst I could cope with non-selection, it was the aspect of being dropped from view altogether that annoyed me. The World squad was, it appeared, excluded from the rest of the squad and their preparation did not include even the reserves of which Colin was apparently one. This being said, I was not privy to budgetary constraints of which I am sure there were many.

Aside from Colin, brother David was about to have probably his finest moment in judo in winning the final contest in the National Senior team's final to secure a 4-3 win for the East against the Midlands whilst the East's ladies' team took bronze. The men's result was not exactly a shock given the strength of the team. But for David it was some comfort for the hard work over the years. He would go on to secure another Irish Senior Open title as he gently fell back from the sport. The cabin was still a venue for training but now David was working for the BJA coaching in schools and his commitment would lessen in time.

The World squad was selected for the German Open and I asked the British Judo Association if they would put Colin in but was told it would be awkward, so I entered him myself. Despite Colin's two wins before being eliminated I knew it did little to enhance his reputation even though few of the team even won a contest. I was running out of options. The list of Colin's 2007 flops was growing, including an early exit at the British World Cup.

It seemed all we were capable of winning were medals at lower-level events in Belgium. We popped back across the Channel in September and took yet another gold medal at -73k at a low-level event but I felt we were really going nowhere and, not for the first time, I doubted whether we could ever win another half-decent international medal.

We had traditionally always entered players for the Irish Senior Open and 2007 was no exception. I was taking a party of players, Colin included. I could tell from my dealings with the BJA that they had probably lost interest in Colin. Whilst I was furious over his treatment in 2007 I really could not blame them; so many chances, yet so many chances lost.

I decided on one last throw of the dice. I could not cancel my trip to Dublin (I had other players fighting in Ireland), which was on the same weekend as the Swedish Open, with the Finnish Open the following week. So Denise and I booked him in for both events back to back. I was looking for a bronze or two to put the pressure back on the BJA to select him again. Luke Preston, the Camberley judo coach, kindly looked after Colin in Sweden and I took over in Finland collecting back-to-back gold medals. I did not experience the one in Boras, Sweden but the feeling in Helsinki was immense. We were back in the frame especially as Colin had defeated Justin Flores of the USA in the Finnish final. This win was significant as Justin had beaten Jean-Rene Badrick at the World Championships in Rio.

Interestingly, Justin beat Colin in the bronze medal final of the New York Open when Colin had a broken thumb and Colin's win was over an injured Justin Flores who was clearly suffering a neck problem in that final. They never met for a third time so we don't know who would have won if both had been 100 per cent fit at the same time. Justin was a fine player.

We flew out of Norwich to Helsinki on a day when the weathermen predicted Armageddon for East Anglia. Apparently the North Sea tides were at a 40-year high, the winds were blowing down from the north and Great Yarmouth was predicted to be under water by noon. You may wonder how many episodes of *Benefits Britain* would have been lost had Great Yarmouth flooded as predicted. (Just kidding, I love Yarmouth and spend a great deal of time on that wonderful coast and especially in the Palace Casino.) So all the flights were delayed, presumably because they were afraid the floods would reach 30,000 feet or so??? We missed our connection but a very kind KLM put us on the next flight. The organisers were aware of our plight and delayed all registrations. Clearly though, the trip was worthwhile.

The back-to-back weekend saw Colin win ten contests in Scandinavia, and the celebrations in Helsinki might have got a little out of hand, to say the least. As a country, Finland is beautiful and the people are great but it is somewhat expensive, as Tom Turner, our heavyweight, discovered when paying £27 for a burger and chips in the hotel. The rest of the Kumo team decided this was too expensive so we went into town to celebrate and have dinner. There was an excessive amount of drinking as well as eating on our tour of the city. It appeared, on our return, that every team at the tournament had joined in Kumo's celebration as the Canadians and the Americans were also in full flow. Indeed, just about anyone who could speak English was wandering the hotel in a very joyful mood most of the night. I doubt very much if anyone achieved more than an hour or two of sleep that night. It was a wonderful example of judo players ignoring nationalism and just having a great time together. I do not think the hotel agreed though as we were never accommodated there ever again. Nonetheless, a fantastic night was had by all. That weekend a certain Ronda Rousey of the USA also took a gold medal. Who could have predicted she would one day appear in a film with the immortal Rocky in *The Expendables*? Can't say I actually noticed her (frankly in my condition that was not too surprising) but then again I doubt she noticed the handsome, if grey, guy coaching Colin throughout the day either.

Two weeks later in December the British Youth and Senior was to be held. At last our opportunity to put the record straight. Jean-Rene Badrick won the youth on the Saturday but did not, for reasons best known to himself or his coach, fight at the senior event the following day. In fairness it would have meant the young man having some 12 or 13 fights in one weekend, not an easy thing to do, but I needed a meeting with him.

The day saw Colin win all seven contests; I think our last encounter with Gareth Carder to take the British crown. The BJA magazine soon managed to put a dampener on any celebrations with the caption underneath Colin's photo in their magazine stating 'Colin Oates took the -66k gold in the absence of Jean-Rene Badrick'. I was livid as any sensitive dad would have been. James Millar had taken the -60k gold but there was no mention of the fact that it was in the absence of Craig Fallon. However, with three gold medals on the trot, it was now going to be difficult to ignore Colin's existence. It now was a case of blaming no one and just delivering the results.

The results of 2008 showed a marked improvement with contest wins in Paris and at the German Super A and, although the Olympics in China was well beyond qualification, we had another shot at the Europeans, picking up a well-earned contest win in the process. This involved a trip to Lisbon, and Denise and I took time out to have a holiday there too. The country was beautiful as were the people.

Around this time I was still looking for quality overseas tournaments and I had heard of one in Lavel which was of such quality that world champions had been known to attend. One of the members of my club, who also attended a club just over the county border in Lincoln, told me that club attended there every year so I asked if he could get the invite for me (if nothing else, to save me getting it off the internet). To my dismay my player came back and told me it was invite-only to special clubs and that they would not help us. With the internet it was actually easy to find and when I did it was deep into France and I thought it was not worth the effort.

The British Senior Open this year was to be held in April, just a couple of weeks after the Europeans.

It was a time of cat and mouse; after working so hard to get Colin back to number one in Britain, should I give his rivals any chance of catching him? In my experience I had found that every time we had fallen behind, our rivals had gone to great lengths to avoid us, either pulling out injured on the day, just fighting up a weight or simply not entering events at all. However, there was unfinished business to attend to; the BJA magazine suggesting that Colin did not really win the British Championship gold hurt.

In the run up to the British Senior Open Colin kept his weight between 66k and 67k. The intention was to fight the same weight as Jean-Rene Badrick. It was nothing personal, I had no axe to grind with him or his coach, but this clash had to happen. It was not a foregone conclusion that Colin would win this fight. I delayed weighing Colin in until the last minute at which point I had confirmed that Jean-Rene Badrick would be fighting -73k. It would have been easy to just move Colin down and play it safe but that was never in Colin's or my mind, so we went -73k.

On the day, a senior BJA administrator was overheard saying they had both gone up to avoid each other. From our perspective nothing could have been further from the truth and that statement amplified just how wrong one-time elite players and British Judo employees could be.

The draw was brilliant as there was nothing I could see on Jean-Rene's side that could prevent him reaching the final. Colin had a tough Portuguese lad at the semi stage, Vladimir Oleinic, and following a really tough contest after which Colin required three stitches in a wound on his head the stage was set for the dream fight of the day. The final was set before the first round was even fought and was to be between the British Senior champion and the British Youth champion. To build the tension, the BJA made that the last final of the day. The stage could not have been better. This was the contest everyone wanted to see. Had they met in an earlier round the result might not have been noticed. Being the final contest of the day there was nowhere to hide. All eyes were on Oates v Badrick.

Walking out to the final with Colin was tense. It was a vital contest and one that could bury a ghost once and for all. I had studied Colin's opponent thoroughly and had watched many of his fights. The instruction was simple: 'not one step into his half of the mat'. If you walked on to Jean-Rene Badrick you were very likely to get thrown. There would be an imaginary line down the middle of the mat and Colin would not be allowed to cross that line. If he did, I yelled for him to back off, as back then you could coach throughout the fight at all levels.

The contest was short-lived as Colin fought the perfect fight, first forcing Jean-Rene to incur a penalty score and then throwing his younger opponent for a winning 10-point score. Colin fought entirely to plan and to my mind it remains one of his best-ever performances There was no more looking back that year as Colin went on to take a gold medal in Northern Ireland and finally broke through at a World Cup with a gold medal in Norway after winning four contests. Colin would reign supreme at -66k for a further ten years. There were no World Championships in 2008; they were held in alternative years at that time.

The Olympics in Beijing came and went, with the British team sadly failing to win a medal, which brought the year to a close. Beyond every Olympics there is always the prospect that players will then retire and, following China, I was unsure what Craig Fallon would be doing. There were rumours he had quit or would move up from -60k to -66k.

We seemed to have seen off most of the players that had threatened Colin's position so we could have been forgiven for relaxing a little.

Following every Olympics there are always changes in sport and the BJA were keen to set up a Centre of Excellence in Dartford. Patrick Roux was going to be the head coach. I was not too worried about this as it seemed a long way off. Our next target was the British Closed in December 2008.

To my horror Craig Fallon appeared at -66k and beat Colin in the final. This was a serious threat and one I did not think, at the time, we could see off. As it happened this was the last real hiccup to our long reign of dominance at the top of British judo at this weight and as Craig seemed to move between the weights Colin was still regarded as the number one 66kg player. Colin ended the year with a gold medal in Finland but, with four years to go before London 2012, we had much to think about with the presence of one of the finest-ever British judo players in our weight category. However, Colin was now winning worthwhile tournaments, defeating world-class opposition, and we were up for any challenge.

THE QUEST FOR LONDON
2008–2012

THE NEXT four years would see the gradual loss of Colin to Dartford and the subsequent demise of Kumo Judo Club as a hub for senior judo players. Under the terms of the condition of being a part of the GB squad, Colin had to spend at least two days a week at Dartford. This was quite a trek for Colin, and over the coming years he went through an assortment of cars in the travel process.

The venue seemed ill-fated from the start but the BJA were starting from scratch. The main problem was asking total commitment yet not providing any future for these young players beyond judo. At one meeting I asked, if Colin committed full-time to the centre, could he do his postgraduate certificate in teaching? This drew a long, blank look and no suggestion as to a solution. There was opposition to the centre's location from many quarters but the dojo was purpose-built and did look impressive.

The internet was now in full flow and not only was it possible to find websites with live results almost as they happened but it was now possible to find live streaming of events. Out in the country, like North Lopham, such streaming was a little sketchy to say the least with contests freezing, usually at a crucial point, but now we, as a family, did not need to travel so much with Colin in order to share the experience. The downside was that, with media and video-sharing channels, there was no place to hide. It was possible to research a fighter you had drawn and study their style. The new age was upon us. I am not too sure when the concept of the forum got into full throttle but the forums began to form throughout the coming years, a place where gutless individuals could hide behind silly nicknames and say things they would not dare say ordinarily. The forums would eventually play a part in a number of aspects involving British Judo.

My involvement as a player ended at the World Masters in Brussels in 2008 with an awful performance that convinced me, at the age of 55, to say farewell to fighting. My preparation of two, maybe three bottles of red wine at my friend Yvonne's house the night before in Stekene probably did not help. If any of my players had behaved in that manner I would have throttled them. But in fact, I realised it was the end when I found myself preoccupied at the arena when working out whether I looked younger than my counterparts. Sadly there were quite a few who had fared better than I had.

The day started quite well with a pleasant drive from Stekene to Brussels on what was a very hot day. It started to go downhill once we reached the venue and discovered that the fighting area was about four flights of stairs upward, not helped by the fact that someone had decided to pass out on them, blocking access. The thought did occur to me that maybe someone else had overdone the wine the previous night.

This now involved almost double the journey to the fighting area, going up, then down stairs in a convoluted manner. Why is it that when anyone passes out or collapses it is usually in the most anti-social position or at an anti-social time? By the time you reached the mats there was no need for a warm-up as you had just completed a half marathon. I received what I thought was a call to the mat and hung around the table with a bunch of guys my size. To my dismay I found they were the -60ks and my group the -66ks were still to be called. When I arrived at the -66ks mat I kind of had an idea of what type of day it was going to be. I started to wonder why I had not cut out the apple pies earlier. The opponents were huge. Now, to be fair, my draw did look good. I was paired with the winner of an Austrian or a German, having the good fortune of a bye to the quarter-finals.

Watching their bout, I got so confident I thought I would take a look at who I would fight in the semi-final, as both the players seemed exceptionally slow and frankly I fancied my chances. Anyhow, it turned out the Austrian won and he was, as I discovered, a former World and European Masters champion.

No problem, I thought; I had done one or two of those types in my time, so I got down to business. The fight was sort of evens; I had conceded an early 5-point throw but things were going okay. Now many will say the three bottles of wine kicked in at the halfway stage and maybe they have a point, as I landed on my stomach just in front of the scoreboard. As I stared at the clock, my head felt like it was splitting down the centre, a headache the like of which I had never experienced. I thought I was going to have a stroke and peg out on the mat in the Belgian heat. However, no self-respecting judo player surrenders that easy. As I stood up I could almost hear the Rocky theme inside my splitting head. I piled into the man with everything I had and what an attack! My grip was perfect, my stance was balanced, my timing was amazing and it was my favourite technique, the fairy-tale Rocky end was there for the taking.

Not quite; this man must have been built like a Russian tank – he did not move. I knew at that point I was, as they say, screwed; the language in my head a tad more colourful. Strange how quickly the Rocky music pans into the Laurel and Hardy theme when it goes wrong. I lost and staggered off the mat, still not sure if a stroke was imminent, to await the German as my next contest. Now, this man was at least 6-foot plus; he must have weighed in minus an artificial leg or two and then screwed them on for the contests. To get an over-the-top grip on him I would have needed a bar stool. My last-ever contest and it must have lasted all of 15 seconds.

Following my last fight and suffering with a headache, I had gone down to the warm-up just to savour the atmosphere one more time. I knew my competition days were done and it is a chapter in your life you have to face at some time. I'm not sure how long I was down there, as I sat there and pondered the good times (that should not have taken that long) and the bad times (that took longer). Eventually I thought it was time to face up to my failure and return to where my wife had been sitting. On walking past the gents' toilets I could see Jack Dennis banging frantically on a cubicle door, calling my name. In Belgium there is generally only one door that separates the corridor from the toilet, unlike the UK. Apparently Jack had been battering this door for ages in the belief I had dropped dead in there. I often wondered what the poor bloke who popped in there to deal with a call of nature was thinking. The only saving grace of the weekend was that of one of my club players, Clare Moore, who battled to a brilliant bronze medal in her category. Sitting in her chair as her matside coach I could lay claim to coaching a player to the club's very first World medal of any sort although I was still comtemplating that imminent stroke.

It was certainly time to quit. I had four British Masters titles and two World Masters fifths so I had done okay. The birth of our first grandson Reece in March 2008 had been a reminder that there was more to life than just judo and, in the years that would follow the London Olympics, it was clear I would wind down on the overseas travel, or so I thought then.

The first event that both Colin and Craig were selected for that year was the Georgian World Cup. Colin took a fifth place with Craig Fallon losing his first contest. On paper it looked like Colin did better than his rival but in reality both lost to the same player, the French man David Larose; there was no advantage one way or the other.

By now I had pretty well team-managed not just the Area Juniors but also the Area Senior squad. In truth this was mainly

Kumo players with one or two exceptions. Kumo was the place to be, especially if you were a senior. The East of England judo committee had financially supported my players, a far cry from the dark early days when I was seen as the bad guy changing everything and annoying all the area coaches. Throughout the years, while David Etchells-Butler was chairman, his committee had shown great support; yes, it is true to say Kumo's input on the committee was maybe a factor. There were still difficult days in the area with a number of, in my view, irresponsible individuals doing what they could to somehow sabotage area business as well as a number of genuine opponents who really did care about the future of the East.

Jonathan Drane (Jono) had now joined Kumo, adding further strength to our mat and giving Colin a great training partner; despite this, the results were still a little up and down. A first-round loss in Paris was followed by a six-contest winning gold medal run at the English Open and a bronze in Lommel, Belgium.

The senior Europeans saw a first-round exit but, more to the point, Craig Fallon did not attend the event; I knew not why.

I had always been very protective of Colin, refusing to let any outside input into his development, but with Patrick Roux the then British squad manager it was different. This man was technically superior to me and I realised that very quickly. More to the point I could see he was taking Colin up a level and developing my son as I had been attempting to, that being with a continental flavour. I knew I had made errors in not focusing enough on Holland and France with our travels but my connections were in Belgium, which had very much developed Colin away from the British style at the time, which was mainly drop shoulder throws.

With Colin at Dartford under Patrick there was progress, especially with the groundwork.

The trip from Norfolk to Dartford was quite a long one, some two hours. Colin had many a nightmare journey back and forth. The car most worth mentioning that he used was an old Ford Escort, known to the family as the clown car. When you turned the steering wheel right the car seemed to go left and vice versa. Needless to say Colin did not make too many trips in that one. The problem was that Colin would go through many old bangers on this punishing run so he too started working as a chicken sexer; he does not mention this often, but it would mean he also had a great party chat-up line if he chose to.

I was now travelling with the Kumo team of seniors whilst Colin was now being sent to some brilliant training camps. A trip to Brazil, countless trips to training camps in Europe – it became clear this type of training could not be organised by a village hall judo club. The centralised system, however much it hurts to lose players, seemed to be the way forward.

The Kumo team was restricted to France, Belgium, Holland and Ireland and, whilst this was good for initial development, it was not likely to win a player major medals.

About this time, world-class start centres were being set up at clubs around the country, and with 12 to 18 seniors on my mat, some 14 or so of them having medalled nationally at some point in time, one might have expected Kumo to be recognised as being just a little above the 'norm'. Such recognition was never forthcoming. I never found out why. Maybe our rural position was a factor or our lack of shower and changing facilities at the hall. In the final analysis it did not much matter, I have always liked to coast under the radar and was not too bothered. The year of 2009 was otherwise a quiet one with Colin taking a fifth at Tre-Torre in Italy and a fifth at the German Open. Denise and myself travelled to Las Vegas for the wedding of my oldest daughter Charlotte to Kumo judo player Sam Webb (who had given me a degree of grief in Philadelphia some years earlier) which distracted us from the judo somewhat. This was a deviation for Denise and I as usually we only ever travelled for judo reasons. It was a welcome opportunity but a costly one as we found a place we loved to visit and a new hobby in playing blackjack.

Colin was selected for the Worlds in Rotterdam where he lost his opener to Niko Niemela of Finland, a player you might have expected him to defeat as he had previous victories over him. It never works out that way and Niko sneaked a famous win and had quite an extended run that day. There was no Craig Fallon at the Worlds again, I am not sure why. At this stage I was unsure of what he was doing; there were rumours he had quit, gone up to -66k, and then back down to -60k. I decided not to pay any attention to what his intentions were but just to steer Colin down the final stretch of the road. Not the easiest of tasks given Craig's incredible ability and the threat he posed.

The World Cup in Birmingham saw Colin place fifth whilst rival Jean-Rene Badrick bowed out early. I was happy that there was now a gap between the two players. I was also mighty relieved the two did not clash in Birmingham as this young man was still a serious threat.

There were more training camps for Colin and we ended the year with another trip to Scotland where Colin took bronze at -73k and a trip to Sweden where Colin took another bronze. This time there was just the three of us: Colin, Jono and me. I had been to Sweden many times before but we found this trip so dull. The competition was great as usual but the town is so dead after dark, sometimes you think they have cleared the streets in the knowledge that the vampires are coming. As for getting a decent pint of beer on a Sunday, there was still no chance as they only sell low-alcohol beer; the question begs, why? I often wondered who actually invented low-alcohol beer and what purpose does it serve?

Colin was gearing up for his first Grand Slam in Tokyo, and to finally prepare the week after Sweden we both jetted off to Helsinki for the Finnish Open. In typical Colin style he took a look at the draw and told me the French boy Frank Sibilo is tasty and what a good O Soto Gari he had. I reassured Colin that he would be no problem. The two met in the second round and, as I predicted, Colin was thrashing him – that was until Sibilo unleashed the throw Colin knew all about. That meant the 1,000 Euros for gold had gone but we were not there for money – it was prep for Japan.

The next contest had an amazing end. Colin was leading by a 7-point throw and in total control against a Russian player when, with five seconds on the clock, the Russian sportingly offered

Colin his hand. Colin moved back as the Russian tried to grab one of Colin's legs. The ruse did not work, but what angered me most was the Russian coach in the chair laughing hysterically. He clearly thought that sort of behaviour was acceptable. As it happened Colin was matched for a bronze medal against another of the Russian coach's players. It just so happened that Colin flew this man with the biggest throw I think I have ever seen. Sadly I retrograded back to my childhood as I leapt out of my chair giving the Russian coach the big one and making all sorts of other provocative gestures at him. Looking back I think I must have been totally mad as he was twice my size and looked twice as mean. At my age I should have known better, not something I would do now.

Sometime during 2009 I actually applied for a job with British Judo as a technical officer. To my amazement I was shortlisted to the last four. I thought the job was to improve judo in the Eastern region as it was titled 'Technical Officer' and remember being floored with the very first question as to how I intended to present the UK Coaching Certificate to clubs. Well, what a shock that was; there I was thinking the idea of the post following the disaster of the 2008 Olympics was to improve judo, and I was actually applying for a job as a UKCC (United Kingdom Coaching Certificate) travelling salesman. I went to the interview not having researched what the job was all about and never stood a chance of an appointment. Well let us not forget the Beatles were turned down by the Decca label and Walt Disney was told he lacked imagination; only a shame I did not go on to make millions as a result of rejection.

Colin's trip to the Grand Slam in Japan was bittersweet. Sweet in that he beat a world silver medallist, Sugoi Uriarte, in his opening fight, and bitter in that he lost to a Japanese fighter in his second, eliminating him from the event. Patrick Roux would show the win on the big screen at the BJA Annual General Meeting which was quite a proud moment for Denise and myself.

As we approached 2010, Kumo seniors Thomas Turner, Emma Paflin and Jono Drane were winning medals at the Commonwealth Tournament in Singapore.

Thomas Turner took gold and Emma and Jono brilliant bronzes. I was woken up in the middle of the night by Tom to give me the news. As a judo coach you are not allowed to sleep if your players are fighting somewhere you cannot be and in a different time zone. Colin took another bronze at the gruelling Belgium Senior Open but made an early exit in Paris. A brilliant performance at the Czech World Cup in Prague saw Colin take bronze and put still more distance between him and his rivals as he was still the only player to have taken medals at this weight, at this level, since the Warren–Sommerville era. The training camps were plentiful and Colin was picking up injuries. He got bursitis in his elbow which hindered his preparation for the Europeans in Vienna, not helped by the flight controllers' strike over France necessitating the BJA having to drive some of the competitors to Austria. Colin lost his opener and went out but he had still remained the -66k number one and, with just two years to the Olympics, that was the most important issue to me.

My wife Denise, who had been on the Area Committee for many years, was elected chairman of the Eastern Area following a close vote of 13–12 from the voting area clubs. It was always likely to be close as people in judo have long memories and we still had those in our area that would have liked to see the family flop. With that vote and the amount of Kumo or ex-Kumo members now loaded on to the Area Committee, it was now unlikely anyone could challenge our control in the East of England. With Denise now the only competition controller capable of running the bigger tournaments, as well as chairman, the opposition I had experienced to the changes I had brought about as the Eastern Area squad manager faded away and I seemed to have won over much of my opposition. Over the coming years we could build the area's competition circuit, attract national events to our base at Thetford (having ditched the University of East Anglia base in Norwich) and produce an Olympian and a Paralympian.

Under Patrick Roux, Colin was now picking up useful World ranking points with fifth places at the World Cup in Madrid and a fantastic fifth at the Grand Slam in Moscow. Tournaments such as Orenburg in Russia which were not point-scoring for world rankings were now events where, if Colin did not medal, they were considered a disaster.

We organised a trip to the Irish Senior Open in Dublin in October 2010 but this was without Colin. The team consisted of Jonathan Drane, who had a bad day (in judo terminology that means he lost his opening contest), and David, who had a slightly better day with a bronze medal. It was a tournament meant to blood our new breed, one of whom was Ben Tippett, a great lad who got a well-earned silver in the youth section.

Throughout the world of judo there are many tales of sacrifice, of how we save money, and this is one of them. To save some pennies we hired only one car even though there were seven players in the team plus me as the driver. We considered we could shuttle players to and from the airport and the competition venue. Ireland was at that time in chronic recession; you needed your credit card to pay for take-out fish and chips. Needless to say every penny saved was vital.

On the return trip to the airport I did my duty and shuttled all but two of the players from the hotel to the airport, leaving only Jonathan Drane and Ben Tippett. When I arrived at the hotel I was greeted by Ben walking to the car in his socks, with my wife laughing, telling me that Ben's shoes had been packed in one of the cases that had gone off to the airport. Ben's reaction was to say, go ahead, tell everybody; in truth you could hardly miss the situation as Ben was a big lad and so too were his feet. Anyhow, we got to the airport and as luck would have it it started to rain. The sound of Ben plodding across the airport car park in his socks will live with me forever. It turned out that Jonathan had decided to pack Ben's shoes away on purpose. It was just as well Ben had a great sense of humour. The trip home was made bearable as the case had not been checked in so Ben changed his squidgy socks and reunited himself with his trainers before boarding our jet.

The following week, Colin, Jono and I jetted off to Sweden where both fought at -73k at the European Cup; the trip proved a disaster as they failed to progress beyond the opening round. Such trips happen to all players in this uncompromising sport. A great deal of expenditure and nothing whatsoever to show for it.

It was in Sweden where I first met Samantha Clark, a fine Scottish judo player, who would many years later with Colin present our family with a granddaughter, Arabella, creating many a dispute as to what accent the new addition would end up with.

As the host nation, Great Britain players did not need to meet Olympic qualification criteria. There was a downside to this as it meant the selections could be subjective and I was still aware of the reputation of Craig Fallon at the lower weight which could still prove a problem to us.

Following the high in Moscow there was the inevitable lull. When Colin returned from a team tournament in Brazil his results dropped off with early exits at the World Championships in Japan, Grand Prix in Holland and the Grand Slam in Tokyo. A fifth place in Korea was the only saving grace on the year end.

We could have been forgiven for relaxing and working out our travel plans for 2012 as Colin was way ahead in the race for the -66k spot in London but yet another sting in the tail was about to hit us. While in Tokyo, following on from the Grand Slam, Colin sustained a neck injury in training that required surgery on his return that would keep him out of the British Closed Trials in January 2011. It had not gone unnoticed by me that Craig Fallon had fought in Sweden in November at -66k and the following week had moved down to -60k, so I was still unsure of his intentions as he had not fought any of the world-ranking events that year.

We turned up at the British trials to be greeted by one of the BJA employees who said to me, with a big beaming grin, 'Fallon's back and at -66k.' To this day I am not sure what response was expected of me, so I just decided to ignore this person who eventually seemed to disappear from the judo scene a few years later as so many do when the pay cheques stop. As expected, Craig Fallon won the -66k group while all Colin could do was watch from the gallery. Did this mean Colin was number two now? I did not think this as Colin's results achieved in 2010 had been impressive and he had built up some world-ranking points. It did mean that 2011 would be crucial and Colin would need something special.

The year of 2011 had begun badly, with Colin recovering from surgery, and his first contest back would be the English Senior Open in March. By now the forums, and there were two main ones, the American one and the BJA one, were up and running with the gutless brigade beginning to 'slag off' anyone and everyone, Colin included. Despite hiding behind anonymity, it was actually obvious who most of these individuals were and where they came from, by who they were trying to destroy with their disgusting posts, and it was even easier to identify what clubs they represented. It was clear to me that I had to keep looking over my shoulder and that of Colin's.

Many of the team selected for the Europeans were under fire from the forums because of their reluctance to put themselves on the line against their rivals in bread-and-butter tournaments such as the English Open. There was an element of truth in what was being said as some players were guilty of avoiding certain events and opponents and in turn aiming to safeguard their positions. It was nothing unusual for judo players and coaches to play these games over the years but now the stakes, London 2012, were higher than normal. The bitterness was evident. The problem was the loudmouths on the forums were probably those players or their coaches chasing the number ones who would have done exactly the same thing had they been in pole position.

So when Colin told me he would do -66k at the English and put himself in the firing line, my first thoughts were that he should follow the actions of many other players and avoid his rivals and fight the next weight up, but on this one Colin got his way and he was right. Colin powered to a hard-earned gold medal, which was great preparation for the Europeans in Turkey. It was Colin's first meeting with Nathon Burns, a rising player more than capable of making an Olympic challenge. However, my eyes were on Craig Fallon who had not fought at the English Open, the player with the huge reputation, an abundance of skill and the heavy forum backing who, at the Europeans in Istanbul, could upset all the world-ranking points Colin had accumulated in 2010.

I could not bring myself to travel to Turkey for the European Championships. Colin and Craig Fallon had been selected at -66k as expected. The prospect of perhaps watching Craig Fallon battle to a medal fight which he was more than capable of doing, whilst Colin may well be eliminated in the early stages, played heavily on my mind. I would not have been allowed matside anyway and the event would be live streamed on the computer. The feeling of depression if Colin blew this one would have been too hard to take so I stayed at home.

In the middle of nowhere, such as North Lopham, streaming was still a little slow which meant the screen would often freeze but I did get to watch Craig Fallon's opening contest, which he lost and, under the competition format, meant he was eliminated. Of course this meant nothing if Colin went out early as well. For the first two contests the stream went down and I had to rely on the live results flashing up which confirmed two wins. His quarter-final fight was against Dan Faisie, a highly skilled player, but at this stage Colin had a guaranteed seventh place which I kept thinking was enough. However, Colin turned in a fine performance to beat his Romanian opponent for a place in the semi-final. Now my brain leapt ahead, thinking the very least Colin would get was fifth. The Olympics looked ever closer. The semi-final saw a defeat against Turan Karimov leaving a bronze medal final against Frenchman Pierre Duprat who had beaten Colin in Holland earlier that year.

It must have been the only time our live stream worked properly, as I watched one of the most gruelling contests I have ever witnessed. At the end of five minutes there was no score and the golden score came into play; another three minutes of hell watching two fighters with nothing whatsoever to separate them. The fight ended and went to the three referees for a decision; the referee in the middle and the line judge on the left of my screen went to Colin, the other voted for Duprat. A split

2-1 decision to Colin, a European medal and world-ranking points lifting Colin into the top 35 of the world. Unless Craig Fallon could produce a medal at the World Championships three months later, we had both feet on the London 2012 mat. Not so according to the internet geek brigade who were now advocating for fight-offs for the Olympics, so ignoring players' achievements in the run in to London, simply because it was not in the favour of their choice. Again it was obvious as to the source of the blogs on the judo forums.

I used to post on the American forum but lost control when some clown again suggested there should be fight-offs and trials for selection; apparently Colin's European medal was still not enough credibility for selection. There was again a certain irony here, as I knew full well Colin was in top spot on performances at -66k at world ranking events but I had always been an advocate for selection by trials. I was in danger of my beliefs biting me in the bum as it could have done with the Egyptian World selections back in 2005. I was so outraged, I posted that all the British team's judo achievements should be ignored and all the players should play darts for their place at London 2012. Best of three, 501 and straight start, double to finish. As to the ladies they should be compelled to appear on *Strictly Come Dancing* and after three weeks Bruce Forsyth should make his recommendations to the BJA. After that post I could not get back on my account again – I think they deleted me.

This power of the net could not, however, be ignored. In addition to attacks on Colin and other prime players, there were countless geeks blogging the solution to all of British Judo's problems on the forums, including the Centre of Excellence in Dartford.

There were stats posted on which centre had more injuries than other recognised centres; it really was so pathetic. It was claimed there were more injuries at Dartford than anywhere else; of course this was totally inaccurate. Why these 'geniuses' hid behind their anonymity if they had so much to offer is anyone's guess as they seemed to hold all the answers. I was staggered by the crass stupidity of some of the suggestions. The one thing evident was that I would have to continue to watch Colin's back and by now I trusted only Patrick Roux, with whom I had a great rapport.

It was apparent to me in April 2011 we had to avoid a head-to-head meeting with Craig Fallon. Colin's record against him was not impressive. I would add that Colin was not fearful of the meeting – it was me playing the tactical games, not him. My youngest son would always fight everyone and anything in his path. A defeat in Hornchurch at the age of eight, another at the BSJA Nationals in Cannock a couple of years later and, as a senior, defeats at the West Country ranking and British trials, did not inspire me that a random fight at this stage with Craig was a good idea. With four defeats and no wins I was not about to take any chances, especially with the forums seemingly hot on Craig's case; we had the world ranking and I was not going to risk credibility with one contest. That would have been irresponsible and I was positive our rivals would never have given us that opportunity had the tables been turned in their favour. Tactical manipulation was commonplace at the time and top fighters often withdrew from events late to avoid that confrontation they did not believe to be in their best interests.

The ensuing months between the Europeans and the Worlds saw Colin travelling to world-ranking tournaments, racking up points along the way, especially in Bucharest where Colin took another World Cup bronze and by now had climbed into the world top 30, just outside what would have been an Olympic qualification place for a non-Briton.

The only times there were likely head-to-head clashes with Craig Fallon were in Orenburg, Russia where Colin moved up to -73k and at the German Open when again Colin moved up a weight to -73k.

As neither of these tournaments carried world-ranking points, Colin could afford to slip up at the higher weight and avoid any likelihood of a head-to-head meeting with any British rival at his Olympic weight. The decision to fight -73k in Germany returned dividends in that Colin defeated Ugo Legrand of France en route to his first-ever German Open bronze medal (only losing to the highly regarded Costel Danculea). Ugo Legrand was one of six victories required to win a medal that day. He was a fighter favoured to medal at the forthcoming Worlds (and in fact took bronze). The selection for London at -73k at that time was between Danny Williams and Jan Gosiewski. Adding Colin to the -73k race was not something we would have shied away from if the going got bad at -66k and, with the forums in full throttle, it was a fall-back plan worth considering as there was little between the three fighters. This being said we went into the World

Championships in Paris relatively confident that we could win at least a few fights and improve the world ranking.

Denise and I made this journey. The draw on paper was not that tough – as if there are any easy draws at a World Championship – but it could have been much more difficult. The pressure, however, was taken off by Craig Fallon's surprise opening-round defeat. Is it horrible to admit I was greatly relieved by this loss? In sport, wishing a loss on a rival might seem harsh, it may even appear that you actually dislike that person but, in essence, nothing could be further from the truth. There were never any personal issues between Colin or Craig or myself. Often you can be close or good friends with a rival but there is usually only one selection place on a team and you may get only one crack at a big event in your judo career.

Colin, on the other side of the draw, battled into the quarter-finals with three wins, only to lose to the defending World champion Leandro Cunha of Brazil. When Colin defeated Igor Soroca to secure a place in the quarter-finals and a guaranteed seventh place, I was not able to contain myself. I leapt out of my chair in the knowledge it was over. A repechage win over Frenchman David Larose and then a bronze final defeat. This meant, with a European third and a World fifth, the Olympics were ours. It was an immense feeling sitting in the stadium knowing there was no way anyone could catch Colin now. The heartbreak of a World bronze defeat almost went unnoticed, as the Games were ours, but there still must be caution as the selection criteria was a little flaky – eventually evidenced by the amount of appeals at the eventual Olympic selection. Just like I argued over Eastern Area junior squad selections many years earlier, when individuals are selecting with subjectivity, they generally cannot be trusted with objectivity. I concede it is not dishonesty; it is human to sometimes go with your heart and not with the facts.

There was one last piece of management left, however, and that was the World Cup to be held in Liverpool. Colin and Craig were both entered at -66k but I advised Colin, who was nursing a strained knee, to pull out close to the event, and some days later so too did Craig Fallon, who announced his retirement shortly after. The meeting of the two that the forums were obsessed about was never now going to happen. My careful, if at times cynical, management had avoided that scenario. A young Lewis Keeble secured a fifth place in Liverpool and with it an Olympic reserve spot in July 2012.

Soon after the Worlds, the British Judo Association parted company with Patrick Roux. It was a very sorry day for us as a family. He was a gentleman first and foremost as well as a brilliant head coach but the lack of medals at the Worlds, the bitter abuse of Dartford on the forums and a number of coaches who constantly made their unhappiness with him well known contributed to his demise. This sacking was a prime example of the aggressive use of the internet. He helped develop my son and brought him to another level that, in my view, no other coach in Britain was capable of doing at that time. When Patrick took over the squads there was no recognised system and even a man of his great ability never stood a chance starting from scratch.

Patrick went on to coach the Russian ladies' team, not what I would have said was a retrograde step.

Colin's 2011 Grand Slam appearance in Tokyo is worthy of mention, in particular his fight with the great Masashi Ebinuma, during which he threw his Japanese opponent for the winning score – apparently, to the satisfaction of the three referees. Even the TV commentary agreed it was a shock win, but it appears the referee in charge was able to overrule the three referees on the mat and bring the players back on the mat. The Japanese guy went on to win the contest and I often have to listen to coaches complain their player was robbed at a novices' competition. I had come so far that I was not angry; my view was that Colin should have thrown him again, he did not so, the fight was lost. My philosophy is, spend more time coaching your player to throw and less time complaining about the opponent's judo or the performance of the referee.

The next nine or so months to the Olympics were a case of keeping our heads low. The caretaker head coach was Daniel Lasco, a man I actually had very little to do with over the coming months; that is not to say I disliked him, he was pleasant enough, but it was a case of just doing what you were told regardless of whether we thought it was a good idea or not so as not to rock any boats.

As 2011 drew to a close, Colin was spending more time at Dartford and less time at Kumo in Lopham. We had the opportunity of sampling the Olympic atmosphere as Jonathan Drane was selected to take part in the Test Event at the ExCel. Even then you could feel the goosebumps – the only difference being you could get a pork pie and get change from a tenner.

Colin and I had gained almost local celebrity status with radio and TV interviews as well as much internet coverage. The local papers were full of the news that an Olympian might be in the making from a rural village.

At the start of 2012 I had a New Year's Day appearance on the Nikki Pryce radio show on Norfolk Radio. By now I was quite used to media attention and I had no fear of a one-hour live radio show. I am not sure how I came to be the family representative – maybe there is truth in that expression of having a face for radio. To that end, perhaps it was a wise move to let Colin do the TV and me the radio. There is always a chance you can slip up on a live show and say the wrong thing and that fear is always in your mind. However, provided you think before you speak, unlike most football commentators or politicians, you usually get by and, as I have spent much of my life watching politicians being interviewed for hours without answering a single question, I too had developed the art of non-committal responses. My years as a Crown Court clerk had involved a considerable degree of public speaking, and live radio was not too different – the only iffy moment being when asked if Colin had a family nickname and I was tempted to swear on radio, but I stood back and said it was not one I could reveal at that time of the day.

There was a trek to Cardiff early in the year for the Commonwealth Tournament where my step-granddaughter Gemma Moore lost in the final to the brilliant Jemima Duxbury in an exciting contest.

Jonathan Drane lost for bronze against Lee Shinkin on what I thought was a harsh disqualification decision. At this tournament, at least the personal coaches were allowed to sit in the chair. Colin, a couple of days earlier, had retained his British crown in what was a busy week for us.

With Colin's position looking solid if not secure, I was able to concentrate on Jonathan Drane and getting him ranked at -73k. He took bronze at the English Open, gold at the Southern Area Open and a further gold medal at the Northern Ireland Open in Belfast. A poor performance by Jono's standards at the British Senior Open was boosted by another great gold medal in London.

In Olympic year, Colin's form was good, as he took another British Championship gold, a fantastic fifth place at the Grand Slam in Paris and toured the World's training camps, just seeming to improve and improve. The selection for the Europeans was a foregone conclusion when disaster struck with an early exit and another injury that would take six weeks to recover from. The Olympics now looked a little less likely. The injury occurred in the team part of the tournament against French player Dimitri Dragin.

Dimitri, realising Colin had been injured, backed away, and did very little in the last 30 seconds of the contest, a wonderful gesture of sportsmanship I will always respect.

The announcement by Craig Fallon of his retirement certainly relieved some pressure on Colin going into 2012; there were still two quality players in Nathon Burns and Lewis Keeble nestling underneath, almost waiting to pounce, but it was the big reputation and sheer brilliance of Craig that I had been most fearful of.

We were told that unless Colin fought the Czech World Cup in June he would be dropped from the Olympic squad; as already pointed out in these circumstances, you did what you were told regardless of whether you thought it was a good idea or not. Colin had already missed a two-week training camp in Japan which was, in our view, not necessary anyway (in fact, I recall punching the air in delight at the prospect of missing Japan), but in the views of those who had the power of selection, Colin needed to prove once again that the -66k number one spot was rightfully his. It was clearly too soon to return to action in my opinion.

Colin won five contests in Prague en route to a brilliant bronze medal. Both Colin and I believed it could be his penultimate appearance at -66k. His opponent that day, Elio Verde, would go on to lose for bronze in the lower weight category. I remember sending him a text saying 'make your last one a medal winner'. I foolishly believed this was one of his last contests at under 66k. Colin was fantastic that day; how on earth could his place have ever been in doubt?

In the run in to the Games, the British squad were treated to an abundance of test fights. Throughout this cycle I failed to see the use of this type of preparation. It seemed to me to be a recipe for disaster waiting to pick up more injuries, especially as some of the team were the other side of 30 years old. Somehow the squad got through, probably more by luck than good management, as did Colin, and as a family we breathed a huge sigh of relief.

The forums still had their dig with one post saying, 'Colin Oates will probably get the Olympics God help us.' I was at a loss to understand why anyone would publicly write such stuff about an athlete simply trying his best. I suppose on a positive, whilst they were attacking us they were leaving alone other more sensitive types who take these opinionated losers to heart. Recent tragic events have shown us over and over how the abusive use of the internet can end; thankfully, not in our case.

As part of the Olympic build-up, the parents of the judo athletes were invited to attend a seminar with free gifts. Yes, yippee, I got something for nothing (mugs and a toothbrush) for the thousands and thousands of pounds I had spent.

Judo players were allowed to nominate a training partner for the Games and for Colin it was clear that should be his brother David. At first we were told this was fine, but then nearer the date, information got back to us that, as they had not been seen training with each other, it was not acceptable. Utter nonsense of course, as if that was any cause for concern. I never did find the true reason but there was probably some selfish motive somewhere, probably to do with the amount of passes allocated and perhaps someone's great granny needed a pass. Who knows? The result was that Jean-Paul Bell would act as both training partner and matside coach, not an ideal scenario. David was quite devastated as you would have expected. He still figured in Colin's preparation and appeared in all the TV coverage. Many years later I discovered, as the host nation, we could do very much what we wanted and there would have been nothing to have prevented David being there. So the question begged, why was David refused as Colin's training partner back then?

The other laugh, or insult, was UK Sport's decision to only allocate tickets to the judo parents for the first session of the day which meant, unless your offspring reached the last eight, as a parent you had to leave the arena and miss the medal matches. Sadly, in the fullness of time, that meant 11 of the BJA teams' parents or loved ones would meet that fate. All the money as parents they had paid to support their kids, the travel and the long days in arenas, and it came down to UK Sport saving pennies in that manner. As one who was fortunate enough to be there in the afternoon, I can confirm there were many, many empty seats that those hard-working parents could have occupied. What a great reward for their dedication! It was another piece of poor behaviour so far as I was concerned.

The day of the Olympics can only be either compared with the birth of your first born or the first time you drink from a bottle of Jupiler beer in Belgium, an experience that will stick in your mind forever. Driving down from Norfolk to my brother's house in Hornchurch, where I knew I could park my MPV safely, I was looking for magpies. Would it be one for sorrow, two for joy? We must have seen about 20 and I don't think the rhyme goes up that high so there was no hint of what was to come there. Colin's draw was an Australian, Ivo Dos Santos, ranked higher than Colin in the world but, without being offensive to the Australian, a contest those in the know would feel Colin could win. Of course, one person wrote on the forum with yet another opinion, Colin could well lose this fight, but now the comments on there were worthless. I no longer felt in awe of any coach in the world let alone the UK; their opinions were actually just that. There was a line in a Clint Eastwood movie that has lived with me for many years, along the lines of: opinions are like backsides (his words a little stronger), everyone has one – that about sums up my attitude to the majority of people I encounter in and out of the sport.

Sadly, we had nothing to follow, as there had not been a single British victory at the Games at that point.

I remember seeing Colin in the tunnel, on the screen, when the situation hit me. As I stared at Colin walking on to the mat with 10,000 spectators cheering through the roof, I began to understand the reality. There had been many truly elite coaches (some of whom had been elite players too) with sons and daughters all competing alongside Colin in their respective categories. Their journey and their goal was always to experience what I was feeling right now, that being the adrenaline buzz of what really would be a once-in-a-lifetime experience for your son and your family – watching Colin Oates fight at the one and only London 2012 Games and soaking up the atmosphere, which still sends goosebumps down my back. That was mine and, of course, that of our supporting family. Both Colin and I had seen off every challenge against all the odds. We did it without the full-time facilities of the so-called World Class centres and without a wide catchment of players to train with, all from a village hall in Lopham in the wilds of Norfolk and a wooden cabin in the back garden.

We would be treated to two wins and the only male member of the British team to place in the top eight of the Olympics, a far cry from the Belgian league days. The first contest against Ivo Dos Santos was as expected a tense tussle and Ivo justified is higher ranking with a solid performance. However, the Olympics is a great leveller and given the difficult circumstances in which our Aussie cousins have to train being out on a limb geographically the fight was anything but easy for him as Colin pecked away with small scores, running out a winner at full time. Dos Santos did not have easy access to the European training camps that are so envied in the judo world attracting players from the former Eastern bloc countries where there are many world class players. Colin had that advantage over his Australian rival and his experience at this level just scraped him home for what was the first British victory of the Games that week. Dos Santos proved to be as tough as we expected and the fight went the full distance. The prize was against one of the tournament favourites for the gold medal.

As Colin stood in the tunnel the threatening figure of Mongolia's Tsagaanbaetar Khashbaater stood opposite him – a fighter who had held the ranking of number one in the World rankings at -66kgs since 2009, had taken the World Championship gold in 2009 and an Olympic bronze at the lower weight of -60kgs in Athens. In addition to having won countless international medals he was also a former World sambo wrestling champion. A place in the quarter-finals was the prize but few in that arena gave Colin any chance in this fight. In their only previous meeting a year earlier in Moscow Colin had been beaten somewhat easily. As the contest progressed Colin fought a rearguard fight, often desperately avoiding some incredible attacks and only the roaring crowd seemed to be keeping the British judoka on his feet. With seconds to go in a fight that had yet to yield a score the Mongolian overstretched and Colin powered him to the floor for a 5-point score. With just four seconds on the clock the elation of an estatic British crowd almost drowned out the sound of the buzzer ending the fight. A seventh place finish was now the worst case scenario and we could look forward to a match with the very much unknown Georgian lad Lasha Shavdatuashvili. Colin would start this as a favourite but how cruel can a sport be? The fight ran to full time with no one having the upper hand and proceeded to three minutes of extra time. The tension in the arena could be cut with a knife. With just seconds to go and a referees' decision seemingly imminent Colin made a blunderous attack and the Georgian secured a pin. It was heartbreaking watching the clock tick down to defeat and the semi-final slipping from Colin's grasp. I always believed rightly or wrongly that had the fight gone to a decision that with the partisan crowd it would likely go to the home player. Now the only medal on offer was the bronze but Jun-Ho Cho, a Korean stood in Colin's way. The Korean had scored two victories over Colin, one in Madrid in 2010 and another in Suwon later that year. He had that style that just somehow made his opponents look bad and Colin never looked like winning that fight. The effort of his first three contests just seemed to have drained everything from his body.

Although the journey was to continue this was the day we probably should have taken a medal – the fine line on the quarter-final loss was the telling factor.

Later that year Wymondham Judo Club would be put forward by the BJA as the Eastern Area club of the year. Even with the East's only Olympic judo player, Kumo Judo Club was still ignored. I would say that Wymondham Judo Club had created a wonderful permanent dojo at the time so I could see why they had been recognised. I was awarded a 4th Dan by the British Judo Association for my services to international judo but, while this may seem like a nice gesture, in truth the 4th Dan was meaningless to me. A letter was sent to me through the post, not even presented at some sort of awards ceremony; one could be forgiven for thinking there was a reluctance to recognise the accomplishment. I won my 3rd Dan on the mat, being battered and bruised and a 3rd Dan I will always remain. I have never sent my licence to be marked and never will. This being said, I do not resent or judge those that gain their grades in this way, simply that it was not my way. We fought for everything we got.

The American forum collapsed soon after the Games and the British Judo Association learnt the harsh lesson not to allow anonymity to idiots on their revised one. This did not stop the creation of the alternative forums, not that I look at them anymore.

I could not sit matside on that special day at the ExCel Arena; this was never going to happen. After all, who was Howard Oates? The answer was always going to be just Colin's dad. The responsibility of the chair went to Jean-Paul Bell. Looking back, would I have made any difference to the result being in my son's chair on that day? As Colin's matside coach I had never lost a medal match at the European level I was allowed to sit at when he was travelling with me. Of course, there is no answer as to whether my presence in his chair would have changed any of the results in a negative or positive way; it is possible he might have lost earlier but my thoughts will always remain with my family on that issue as to what I believe. What was certain, in not having David as Colin's training partner or myself in his chair, some 25 years of personal knowledge about that athlete was without any doubt lost and the margin of the quarter-final loss was minimal. David was the oracle of judo and had vast knowledge on the Georgian's style. In fact, I fell further away from involvement in Colin's judo as he went on to even greater achievements post-2012 together with Jonathan Drane. David went on to work for British Judo as schools' coach for some years before eventually qualifying as a schoolteacher; obtaining that degree years earlier proving very useful and a warning to all young judo players that education should not be ignored despite what some individuals in British Judo may have echoed at the time. When you stop winning medals there is still the rest of your life, and sadly the medals you have won are generally not sufficient to put a roof over your head.

The stress of being a father and a personal coach had left its mark; I have serious doubts that the two are compatible.

It is unlikely anyone in the future will be able to retain interest in a player developed from grassroots, such as we did to the Olympics, with the present system as all elite players are expected to train at the Centre of Excellence in Walsall. So unless you have pots of money or live in the close proximity of wherever the Centre may or may not be, most clubs will lose their players at a relatively early age. Personal coaches, it appears, will have less and less input in real terms the longer the system is in place, their primary function being only in the development of cadet or junior players in the modern age, unless a player is fortunate enough to have sufficient money and can self-fund events. It is not just a case of paying for travel to competitions but also having private health insurance in case of injury and perhaps even having a sports psychologist too. So the Centre of Excellence certainly makes the process cheaper for the personal coach as it means, if your player has the potential, the Centre will take over the travel costs which nowadays are very high. Despite at times feeling I was edged out, I agree with the system of central development. It is true to say I was affluent enough to travel with and pay for many of my sons' and daughters' overseas trips, but there must be many, many others not so fortunate, yet maybe more gifted.

If the journey had ended in 2012, we as a family would have been more than satisfied with our contribution to British judo and the history we made. The coming years would see less of my contribution to Colin's technical judo, as a new system and structure began the process of trying to get the centralised system in a new place and to be more successful.

THE ROAD TO RIO 2012–2016

THERE WAS a sense of achievement following the London Games but also a hollow feeling. We had reached a loose agreement that Colin would perhaps carry on to the next biggest multi-games event in the World, the Commonwealth Games in Glasgow in 2014, and retire. We had discussed the possibility of moving up a weight to under 73k and pumping into the category. What was clear was that Colin would move out of Lopham to a Centre of Excellence if he intended to continue competing at the highest level. Kumo Judo Club still had a number of quality players, especially in Jonathan Drane who had all but replaced David Oates as Colin's main training partner. However, Kumo was clearly in decline as most of the players were getting older and falling away from the sport and there were few players likely to replace them. It was also inevitable we would lose Jonathan to a Centre of Excellence as well as he too progressed to Rio.

Over the next few months Colin had the opportunity to wind down. He still attended Dartford, where his good friend Ben Quilter was preparing for the visually impaired section of the Paralympics. Ben was to delight the crowds with a fantastic bronze medal. Beyond that, Colin took a lads' holiday, his first in years, to Turkey, the country where he launched his first World bid with a bronze medal at the European Cup.

Colin's departure from Norfolk was very low key. Although he had announced he would head to Scotland and train full-time at Ratho in Edinburgh, when he finally loaded his car with his possessions, he never actually said as he drove off that he was leaving home. I still remember the day as I watched him head off; I knew the truly close-knit judo partnership would never quite be the same.

Over the years I had been accused by many of carefully managing a judo player who was technically limited. I have to admit there was a time when I was somewhat hurt and offended by these allegations, preferring to be regarded as a half-decent coach. However, now I took the role far more seriously. It was not likely that I could have any more serious technical input into coaching Colin, some 400 miles north of me, but I certainly need not lose sight of the managerial aspect.

With Colin living in Scotland, it was also clear we would have a place to stay for the Commonwealth Games and at the Great Britain European Opens, which were being staged in Glasgow. So from my perspective it was a winning situation even if the trip up was a long one. I had also grown tired of my travelling to and from Heathrow and Gatwick to take and collect Colin from squad activities. Although I received my mileage from British Judo, it was a five-hour round trip minimum to each airport, so in real terms each journey took up a day of my life, and sitting in a car for five hours plus on a Friday and then again on the Monday was not too pleasant, even though my Toyota Celica often used for those journeys was a joy to drive. There were nightmare journeys on the M25 due to the widening scheme where we would be constantly looking at the clock, stuck in traffic, and hoping above hope we would not miss the outward flight and cost the BJA extra money. As it happened we never did miss a flight but there were so many close calls way beyond our control.

Colin made the decision to stay at -66k rather than move up a weight as it might have compromised his UK Sport funding. This was not a direction I favoured but I could see the sense in Colin's decision. Over the next few years we would see the emergence of the 'self-funded' players on a major scale and this route was hardly a cheap option. Our decision to continue at the same weight had more to do with the financial side of matters than a desire to stay in the weight. The prospect of chasing a sport with little prize money, nor sufficient celebrity status that you could even guarantee a job as a media pundit on retirement, did not appear to be a sensible approach. Without sounding offensive, some British sportsmen who won absolutely nothing major in their careers worthy of mention could find themselves on television. In the case of ex-judo players, few have found a status worthy of their dedication or efforts.

In a nutshell, judo in the UK is a minority sport where, in our view as a family, the huge investment of large sums of money is not shrewd, as there is little chance of any worthwhile financial return. That is not to say that we ever sat in judgement of those players, parents and clubs that have piled thousands of pounds into the sport. We too had our moments, but the events we sponsored years earlier were as a family and we took the opportunity to travel the world and have a great deal of fun together; it was not just about judo – our trips bonded us as a family and as a club. The prospect of funding an event simply to score Olympic qualification points is a scary, if bold, prospect. I can think of nothing worse than paying a huge amount of money and then risk drawing the one player I wanted my athlete to avoid and be eliminated before the latter stages. I cannot comprehend the depression of such failure.

This being said, in the sport of judo a degree of investment is always necessary. Following the Olympics I was able to focus on Colin's training partner Jonathan Drane. He had helped me plumb in all the bathrooms in my house and would not take a penny for it. Quite frankly, he was one of the kindest individuals I had ever come across. I was hoping to repay him by helping him qualify for the British Senior Trials. The BJA, over the years, have changed the qualification criteria many times, but in 2013 a player had to finish in the top 16 of Britain. This meant, just like a rock band, going back on the road again and touring the ranking circuits. Given that, with Colin in Scotland, I would be spared all those horrid runs to the airports, I could turn my attention to travelling the length and breadth of Britain yet again and over the next few years I did exactly that.

Following Colin's Olympic quest, I knew he would return to the competitive circuit with a flat performance. He had been picked for an amazing tour whereby he would fly via Australia to Fiji for a Continental Open before travelling on to Korea for a Grand Prix. Unfortunately I had already picked and booked his comeback event at a Continental Cup tournament in Malaga, Spain. There was a somewhat selfish motive on my behalf, as, over the years, most of these tournaments had been held in cold countries like Finland and Sweden and the events were all held in wintertime. With an event in Spain, I, for once, was in my element with sun, cheap wine and judo. What could go wrong? Well I had to get Colin back to the UK almost directly after the tournament so that Denise could shuttle him off to Heathrow for his Far East tour. We did the business with the flight arrangements and so Jono and I flew to Spain from Southend airport and Colin met us in Spain, having flown direct from Edinburgh. For me, flying from Southend was a somewhat surreal experience as I remembered flying from that very airport on a propeller-driven Vanguard aircraft for a football tournament in Ostend. As a 17-year-old I could never have imagined flying out with one of my judo players some 42 years later on a jet.

Colin lost to a player he would have been expected to beat in the under 73k category; that is in no way intending to take any of the glory from Tjeerd Tjeerdsma who beat him. Sadly, Jono, not for the first time, was the victim of two close fights decided by referee decisions that could have easily gone in his direction. An expensive weekend that was to yield no worthwhile results but it did blow the cobwebs off both players who needed a run out.

That evening I thought I would compensate myself with the red wine that appeared to be on tap and free whilst Colin jetted back to the UK (not before losing his printed boarding pass and having to pay an extra £60) and Jono went off to the town with the Scottish team.

It was in Malaga that I realised I had achieved some level of respect when I was approached by an English coach, who had clearly found the on-tap free wine and told me everyone thought, and I quote, 'That you were a ******* prat but you did it.' Oddly I was quite flattered by this somewhat perverse compliment, presumably about getting Colin to the Olympics, and the guy talking to me clearly meant it with affection.

The tour on the other side of the world was a relative success with a silver medal in Fiji following a split-decision defeat in the final against Kamal Khan-Magomedov of Russia and a fifth place in Korea.

The year of 2012 ended and what a year it had been. It spelt the end of Dartford as the squad base and a new team was in the process of being set up as Walsall emerged as being the place where the squads would be relocated. Gemma Gibbons, who had taken a fantastic silver medal at the Olympics, had or was in the process of relocating to Scotland, as had Colin, so Dartford was losing many quality players.

The next event Colin would compete in was the British Nationals to be held in January. It proved an unpopular choice of dates, being shortly after the New Year festivities. Many athletes felt they trained hard enough throughout the year with few breaks and believed that the Christmas period should have allowed the players to unwind a little. The day was a total disaster for Kumo Judo Club with Jono reaching the last four and a guaranteed medal, only to be disqualified for an alleged punch in his last match to lose his medal, and Colin dropped an early pool defeat against Chris Waddell, which on the countback system meant he would only take silver – a system that saw Colin with five wins against one defeat in silver place and Chris with four wins and two defeats in the gold spot.

Despite this situation I still believe this is the best trials system and Chris thoroughly deserved his gold medal that day. There is one bone of contention; despite the countless British Nationals victories Colin has secured, the first one that our governing body had managed to stick on a social media website was the one he lost against Chris. It has attracted a huge amount of hits too. I have to admit, if that had been my son beating Colin, I think I might well be guilty of watching it on a daily basis. I would also add that British Judo have indeed more than redeemed themselves, and I must say they have since put many wins from Colin on there now. The trip back from Sheffield to Norfolk was also a nightmare as most of us driving south were heading into blizzard conditions which, coupled with a number of turkeys in apparent control of a vehicle, proved to be one difficult run home.

The disqualification of Jono at the British Trials spelt the end of my road trips around Britain attending senior ranking events (or so I thought at the time). I probably took that defeat worse than Jono; all the effort and time I had put in, let alone Jono taking it on the chin so to speak, and to lose a medal in that manner was hard. Jono was in any event developing into a visually impaired player where he clearly had a better future. He would go on to take a bronze medal at the World IBSA visually impaired championship and qualify his place for the Paralympics in Rio where he would come so close to a medal. As with Colin, I would not be any part of the process of Jono's future development nor would I ever be in his chair for a major event again but it was not about my ego. The only issue that mattered was getting the best for those athletes.

I had, since 2006, realised that, as a personal coach, your involvement would fall away once the player had reached an elite level. Over the years I had travelled across Britain, Europe, Africa and the USA with Colin and Jono, mostly at my expense, and it would have been nice to have been more involved; however, both stayed very much in touch over the coming years. In future I intended to function only within my local area and, without my travelling players, that should have been easy.

The British trials was the last event Colin would do for some time as he needed rectifying surgery and would be unable to fight for another six months. The timing was not good as the Commonwealth Games qualification criteria had been set and Colin was out injured, leaving his main rivals Nathon Burns and Lewis Keeble an opportunity to build up a points lead. We were now emerging into a new phase of travelling judoka whereby, as long as you were a squad member, you could pay to enter world-ranking tournaments that you once had to be selected for, and these events formed part of the Commonwealth Games selection process.

Colin had missed a number of events that ordinarily he would have been selected for. He was not likely to be fit for one until a Grand Prix in Miami. Unfortunately both his rivals had booked the only two spaces reserved for the Great Britain team, effectively squeezing him out; at the time I was not entirely sure it was not a cynical and deliberate move to squeeze Colin out. Even if Colin could get on the trip we were told by our governing body that we would have to find the £1,500 cost. Our governing body had saved money that they would have ordinarily spent on Colin to do a number of events that he was unable to compete in as a result of his surgery, so one would think logically they had money that could have been spent on him later; evidently not as it turned out. In truth you never actually know how the system works; I am sure if British Judo could have helped they would have but this time we were on our own.

The future looked quite bleak at this point. I did get the impression that there was a belief on the circuit that Colin had passed his sell-by date. Both of Colin's rivals were more than capable of taking a medal at the coming events which would have given them a headstart on what was likely to be our final target at the Glasgow Commonwealth Games.

As it happened, one of our English rivals sustained an injury at the British Open, I believe, and had to pull out of both Miami and the Continental Open in San Salvador. I had to keep one eye on the idea that some clubs, players and coaches had clearly worked out that, by booking Grand Prix places in advance, it was possible to freeze a rival out of competing and prevent them scoring the required ranking points. Indeed, I suspected this might be the case and, as by now I trusted no one, I had to keep vigilant and even look beyond this event. However, we were in luck; one of the places became vacant so any cunning plan to prevent Colin competing was scuppered by an injury, giving us the opening. Kumo Judo Club, Colin and the Eastern Area region all contributed £500 each and the trip was on – an opportunity to put points on the board for the swansong Commonwealth Games in 2014.

If all sporting careers went the way of a Sylvester Stallone Rocky movie it would be wonderful; alas that is never the way. Colin dived out in Miami but went on to take a silver medal in San Salvador but, more to the point, immediately placed himself in pole position at the top of the Commonwealth selection rankings.

There was an ulterior motive to the American tour; it was not just about Commonwealth Games selection. The governing body had told Colin his first funded event back was going to be the Grand Slam in Moscow, an awesome tournament. Quite frankly, to even think it was a good idea to have had nearly seven months out and come back with a tournament. of this magnitude was, as far as I was concerned, a bad idea to say the least, and I would have been failing Colin had I sent him back without a warm-up event. Moreover, I started to think perhaps, at 30 years old, there was the belief in British judo that he was beyond further investment, not an unreasonable viewpoint, and an inevitable failure in Russia would have sealed an end effectively to his career. Many scenarios fly through your head. Out in Malaga I had told Colin that, post-2012, anything he got would be a bonus, and so far we had tucked up two Continental Open silvers and a Grand Prix fifth place.

Colin had never medalled at a Grand Prix or a Grand Slam, and when I saw his draw against an excellent Russian I feared an early exit. The Russian had won that Grand Prix in Miami and had lost just twice in two years; in fact, I doubted my own son so much that I overslept, and when I got up in the early hours of the morning to watch the event unfold Colin had already won his opener. It was a case of £1,500 having been well worth the effort as Colin won a great semi-final against Nijat Shikhalizada in the sudden-death golden score time. He lost the final to Charles Chibana of Brazil but the medal all but ensured the Commonwealth Games, such was the points gap on his rivals after this performance, and lifted Colin into the top ten in the world. Suddenly, 2016 and Rio was within our sights and, with the Commonwealths all but secured, we could look to more Grands Prix and Slams as we weaved our way toward that second Olympics we had never planned on.

It seemed Colin had saved his best for his veteran years, but I still believe, had we not done the American tour, the Grand Slam in Russia would have resulted in a first-round defeat and that would have been his likely swansong. To my mind, this was a case where the player did truly need careful management from a personal coach.

Since the Olympics, the governing body had introduced stringent selection criteria, and when I first saw them I took the view they were very unfavourable to the older player, and they were in fact reviewed – whilst many still disagreed with the process, at least they were transparent. The Grand Slam silver in Russia secured Colin's place in Rio for the World Championships.

Hopes were high as Colin approached the Worlds, until we saw the draw. The only way it could be described was, as the draw from hell. Colin's task was simple; all he had to do was to beat a two-time Olympic bronze medallist, Rishod Sobirov. Once past him, Colin could face his London conqueror and Olympic champion, Lasha Shavdatuashvili. The fight with Sobirov was a tense affair with Colin needing a golden score yuko to secure an unexpected victory, so much unexpected that someone wrote in the comments section of a media website 'OMG Sobirov lost.' This victory set the scene for a rematch with the reigning Olympic champion. Unlike the fight in London there was no need for a golden score, as Colin gained sweet revenge (I would have still preferred to have lost this one and won the London meeting) with a great 10-point score for a place in the last 16 against surprise player Azamat Mukanov.

After disposing of two Olympic medallists, we had high expectations of at least placing, but in this sport everything that can go wrong often does, and the fight was over almost before it started. No amount of training can legislate for a great throw. Mukanov went on to take a silver medal.

Despite the disappointment, it was on to Croatia for a Grand Prix and Colin's first Grand Prix medal, a bronze – that could have been a better colour medal had there not been a semi-final error. When Colin was walking out for these International Judo Federation finals, they were still showing my name on

Ippon TV as his coach, and I thought this was a nice sign of appreciation of all the work I had put in over the years but, somewhat cynically, I did ponder on how long that recognition would last and, sure enough, as the medal finals began to roll in my name was removed and substituted. No explanation was ever given or indeed sought by me; I think I knew it would happen eventually. Frankly, perhaps during this period, maybe I should have checked Colin's birth certificate to see if I was still named as his dad.

The Asian tour to Abu Dhabi, Korea and Japan was nothing short of a disaster – not just for Colin, but for the touring British squad, most of whom were probably tired from a tough post-Olympic year. In Colin's case he only managed to register one victory over the three events. Strange to think, had the results occurred 18 months earlier the geek brigade on the judo forums would have been throwing out insult after insult at Colin in the pursuit of their own agenda, whatever that may have been. Now with no Olympic selection and the onset of forums where one could not hide so easily behind anonymity, critics at this stage were decidedly more passive. Moreover, that squad had not performed as a team and critics of Colin would have needed to tread carefully as to the rest of the other athletes' reputations too.

The British Championships had been scheduled for the middle of December rather than January. It did mean there were two National gold medals begging in his weight category in 2013. The date change was very helpful as it meant the athletes could enjoy the festive period without the worry of making weight early in the new year.

Maybe, given Colin's poor performance on the Asian tour, there was the option for another -66k player to shine and take over his number one spot; however, seven emphatic victories secured the British Championship and gold medal, more Commonwealth Games qualification points, as if they were needed, and a caveat to the rest of the field that Colin was still the British number one. Oddly, none of Colin's seven wins that day appeared on any social media website as the loss to Chris Waddell did earlier in the year.

By now I had grown tired of taking the old video camera so I was actually hoping someone had filmed his day.

At those British Championships I was not a validated coach anymore; my criminal record clearance had been delayed, through no fault on my part, so when I arrived and tried to gain access to the competition area that day I was told I was not eligible as I was not a coach. Argue as I did, the official would not let me enter the arena. Now let us think about this; I had guided my son from an under-eight competition in 1989 to the London Olympics in 2012 travelling the world over, having been a qualified coach some 20 years and suddenly here I was being denied a coaching pass? Fortunately I had a last trump card up my sleeve. I simply told them I would have to explain to the BBC why I could not commentate on Colin's fights for Radio Norfolk. Eventually they gave me a pass, such is the power of the BBC, and I had the task of commentating on judo contests for radio, not so easy, but I coped okay. The only real problem was during Colin's scrap with Jamie McDonald when, just at the point where I said Colin seems to be in control, Jamie threw

Colin for a huge throw; fortunately for us, Colin managed to pin his opponent and win the fight. Jamie's brilliant throw, however, made my commentary somewhat laughable.

As the year turned, focus, as far as I was concerned, was on the Glasgow Games. It certainly was not, however, high on the list of priorities as far as Colin was concerned; he was stalking glory at European or World level. By now under the new system, I had no control or contact over Colin's coaching development nor was I involved in what tournaments he should be doing, but I still felt the need to manage his career as I had since he was five years old. I was well aware that the media coverage on the Commonwealth Games would far exceed that on winning a Grand Slam medal as he did in Russia; that performance barely got any coverage in the media. As Colin progressed into the veteran years as a player it was vital to keep a high profile in case there may be opportunities arising as a result. I saw the Commonwealths as a real opportunity to keep Colin's name out there.

2014 was meant to be the final competitive year for Colin Oates, but sitting in the top ten of the world meant the show was likely to go on, and why not? We had broken new ground with a Grand Slam and a Grand Prix medal and had started to defeat players of the highest levels. Long gone were the days when the first major international Colin would have to confront would be the gruelling Belgium Open – now we could look forward to selections for the Grand Slam in Paris. Whereas once selection was an iffy process, now it seemed selection for the big competitions was a foregone conclusion.

It was a wonderful place to find ourselves after many years of uncertainty.

This did not mean the medals were guaranteed, and the year began the same way the previous one had concluded. This time, with an unexpected defeat against Tal Flicker; again, this is not to distract from Flicker's win but Colin had beaten players many rungs higher in the world than Flicker. The win would, in my view, be considered at that time to be one of Flicker's best results.

It is fair to say he went on to record many other fine wins too including a further victory over Colin to become the number one ranked player in the world in August 2017 and take a World bronze medal.

Since the very first tournament Colin had fought in back in 1989, technology had made amazing leaps. We now had a situation where individuals on social media could boast about having hundreds of friends, I assume as long as you did not ask then to lend you a tenner until the weekend. Those on such sites could, I understand, find out whether their friends were happy, sad, in a relationship or not in a relationship, as the case may be, simply by turning on the very phone you could use in place of that massive video camera I once used to record Colin's second tournament in 1990.

Then we had tweeting, and the advent of hearing on the news what some celebrity would tweet after hearing of the death of some other celebrity. As a family, we even celebrated a Christmas dinner with, it seemed, nobody talking to each other, but simply texting the person opposite to ask them to pass the mint sauce (only wish I was joking).

Perhaps this was the stage of my life I realised that I was fast becoming a dinosaur in danger of extinction. It was great that I could watch Colin fight via a live stream on my laptop but did I need to know Ricky Gervais's tweeting views on religion or in fact anything else he has to say for that matter every time a celebrity died? However, desperately trying not to get like my old nan who died in 1972 but even then did not understand how to play records on our radiogram, I made the effort to be with it and I followed what fighters tweeted. Frankly, at times, I wish I had gone down the same road as my nan and not bothered. I wondered whether, the authors of such tweets or postings really believed what they were saying.

To be fair, I knew so many of the fighters and they were all both likeable and modest and certainly dedicated and, in a world where their incredible dedication was not in my view recognised, I can only believe they had to paint some of those pictures of themselves on the social media sites to attract sponsorship. Over the years I also considered some players chased dreams a shade too long and, as with my other offspring, David, you have to be aware that there is a life outside this sport. I was fortunate all my sons and daughters knew their limitations without my input. I would always advise every player in my club to lay a foundation for a life after judo and had no reservations on telling them the truth as to the reality of their aspirations.

I remember a prominent figure in our Association making a statement that our players were lacking in dedication simply because there were some that had chosen to gain an education whilst training. I thought this view a little short-sighted given the failure rates of so many of our truly talented athletes. Where do elite judo players go at the end of a career? There is life after judo and to ignore that reality is reckless. In the present climate there is quite rightly emphasis on the mental health of retired athletes; little wonder there is a problem when mixed messages about obtaining an education to ensure a future beyond the sport are being echoed.

There was an emergence of websites through which you could make a donation to a player, usually one who was not being funded through their national governing body. These websites were a work of genius, as the creator would take a percentage or cut of what was being donated, so it was a nice little earner for those individuals behind such sites rather than a real effort to help struggling athletes. What really shocked me was the fact that it was not just a sport thing; it seemed you could get a fund-me website for just about everything. If you had a dream, an aspiration, a project or an ambition, all you had to do was ask online for money. And not just a loan like you might get from your friendly bank manager but an absolute gift. If ever I felt I was born in the wrong time? I started to think it might be worthwhile starting a crowdfunding site to raise money to purchase the Dodge Charger I always promised myself.

British Judo had performed above the target set for medals at the London Games but, despite promises from the politicians that funding would not be cut, the goalposts were moved.

Sadly our Association was having to make cutbacks, one of whom was David who, employed as an Enjoy Judo coach, was made redundant – he used the opportunity to train as a school teacher. There were many other good people, not so fortunate sadly, who had to go but, without getting carried away on sentiment, there were one or two I was glad to see the back of as, with any big organisation, you do not get on with everybody. The light at the end of the tunnel being that a good number had gone off to ruin another sport they had no real interest in.

As judoka in the UK approached the run in to Rio it became clear that British Judo did not have the money to fund all the athletes they would like to have done, so the reality was that many would have to beg, borrow or steal. Colin and I had already made the decision prior to the Glasgow Games not to invest any more money on judo tournaments. In the real sense we had only ever gone down that route once and that had in effect probably saved Colin's career.

The period between 2008 and 2014 also saw the emergence of the academic coach where there were even university courses in the sport. We also found ourselves in the age of the high-powered titles. There were individuals calling themselves performance coaches, high-performance coaches, elite coaches; it seemed everybody had a fancy title. I once saw someone at a competition with 'Head Coach' written on his tracksuit top, severely tempting me to get one made with the words 'Big Head Coach'. Not being someone who ever took myself seriously, I think I have difficulty with overuse of the word 'elite' in any context.

During 2014 it was clear that Colin's body was taking punishment but the best was yet to come in. He started 2014 with another win over Rishod Sobirov in Paris but then bowed out to Masaki Fukuoka of Japan, and then exited in the first round of the Grand Prix against Tal Flicker (yes, him again) – not exactly fighting form in qualifying for the Rio Games. However, then came the purple patch and a great bronze medal at the Grand Prix in Turkey. Hopes were high at the European Championships in France but a frustrating defeat against Loic Korval saw Colin eliminated. Loic would go on to take gold. Colin held Loic for 24 seconds – one second away from victory (and in modern rules an outright victory, as 20 seconds wins the contest) and then got thrown with three seconds on the clock – such is the margin between glory and disappointment.

In Baku, Colin had his finest moment when becoming one of very few British men to boast of being a modern-day Grand Slam winner when beating the tough Russian Kamal Khan-Magomedov. And what tactics had Colin employed? He deliberately gave away two cheap penalties to slow down Kamal's attack rate and lull him into sitting back on his lead, as back then you could win on penalties. Kamal did just that, allowing Colin to dictate the pace of the contest and go on to win it. Suddenly with a mass of Olympic ranking points Colin was back in contention and had thrown down the gauntlet to his main British rivals to catch him. We were back on track for yet another Olympic Games.

The process was not to be repeated at the Grand Slam in Russia where we were treated to some unusual officiating both against Russian players (in Russia, I say again) but that is judo, where the only way to guarantee a win is to keep throwing your opponent.

Colin had wrapped up the Commonwealth Games selection at a very early stage and the event was one with the pressure of anything less than gold being a disaster. How crazy a situation was that? Here I was, the man from the village hall club in the back of beyond, a coach that had not any elite competitive experience as a player and now at the Commonwealth Games it was a case of the player I had guided taking a gold or we would consider the day a disaster. It was not arrogance – we had this pressure because at the time Colin was ranked in the world top ten.

Judo at the Commonwealth Games requires some explaination. In not being, until recently, a core sport the host country could remove it and add a sport that is likely to yield more medals for their athletes. Our sport first featured at the Commonwealth Games in Edinburgh in 1986 and has popped in and out ever since. To ensure there is Commonwealth interest in judo there is also a tournament that is held every two years other than a year when it might feature at the major Games. Colin had already won the Tournament version in Ireland in 2006 but this time the event would be part of the second-biggest multi games in the world after the Olympics.

We drove up to Scotland in the same Toyota Ipsum that I had taken to the London Games. Most athletes and coaches all seem to have tried and trusted traditions and do not like to shy away from them in case it causes bad luck. The day of the event still seems a little surreal if only because Scotland was experiencing a heatwave.

Unlike London there was not any player we truly feared; by now Colin was an established class player. The draw was still tough though and the young Canadian lad Antoine Bouchard was on our side of the draw. I had done my homework and was well aware of this man's obvious class. He would go on to win three Pan American Championships, and lose painfully for bronze at the Rio Olympics en route to countless international medals. I feared he was a real threat but he was surprisingly defeated by Narna Etoga Dieudonne of Cameroon. In judo shock results are not uncommon.

My gameplan for Colin was to take no chances. When fighting players not as experienced there is always that chance that you can get thrown and this is where most shocks happen as in the case of the Canadian so Colin was under instruction to take his first opponent to the ground as soon as possible. On the ground it is far less likely you will make an error and indeed the plan worked a treat on Mohd Fikri Mohd Farhan Uzair of Malaysia and Colin and my tactics worked a treat.

Next up would be the current Indian and reigning Commonwealth Tournament champion Manjeet Nandal. India is not renownwed for producing judo players but in wrestling they are certainly a powerhouse and most Indian judo players will have a history in wrestling. So again caution was the order of the day and Colin again tumbled his opponent to the ground where his amazing skills in this area carved out a victory.

James Millar defeated Narna Etoga Dieudonne to set up the dream semi-final between Scotland and England. Colin had a good record against James but there was always a danger with James – a man that once qualified for the Olympic Games but was pipped to the spot by Craig Fallon. My thoughts were now on how would the home crowd respond to Colin when he took to the mat against the home favourite? Any concerns I had were ill founded as both athletes received a magnificent welcome. The wonderful aspect of judo is how we seem to ignore nationality, something evident at international training camps. Colin duly beat James in a tense battle with a couple of low-scoring throws and won a place in the final.

Later in the day we were now left with the prospect of James fighting in what was to be his last top-class contest for a bronze medal. Could James gain a little piece of the history he so richly deserved? The answer was yes and James took a well-earned medal. Yes I was delighted for him but something did not seem right. Earlier in the day I had been cheering for another Scotsman, John Buchanan, when he fought in his last top-level contest, again for bronze at the lower weight. I am not sure I can ever forgive either of them for getting me, an Englishman, to cheer on a couple of Scots guys. Some years later my wife Denise did an ancestry DNA test on me and it transpires I am 81 per cent Irish, Scottish and Welsh (we will not go into the remaining 19 per cent) and, as I was born in England, it appears I can claim all parts of the UK, if that is ever something that matters anyway.

The final was against Andreas Krassas of Malta who was ranked considerably lower than Colin in the world rankings. Often in judo you can beat players higher on the list yet lose to some much lower. The gameplan was again to take his opponent to the ground as soon as possible to avoid any possibility of a standing error allowing Krassas the one opportunity to get a throw into the mix. After just two minutes Colin threw the Maltese lad for a small score and followed up with an instant armbar forcing a submission. The legendary British icon, double Olympic silver medallist, four-time World medallist and five-time European champion and voice of judo commentary Neil Adams described Colin as the master tacticion on television. A compliment we cherish to this day.

With a Commonwealth Games gold medal in the bank, the inevitable media attention followed with television interviews; as I expected, the media were totally sold on the performances of all the British judo athletes at the Games without perhaps realising that many of those medals should have been and were foregone conclusions. This being said, there were a few shocks. Anything less than gold for Colin would have been a deep disappointment. Colin was by far the highest-ranked fighter in his category and had every right to expect to win it. I just wish Colin could have done the backflip celebration that John Buchanan performed after his bronze win – no man of that age should have been able to do that and live to tell the tale.

At the end of the year, Colin went on to take another Grand Prix medal, this time in Korea, his first and only success on the Asian circuit, always a tough one. All the while the ranking points were solidifying Colin's place in Rio.

As we moved to the end of 2014 I began to consider what Colin would do post-Rio. As I have already said, the prospect of him being picked up by the media was quite remote. I had seen how professional agents had marketed other members of the British squad and was, to say the least, very impressed by what

THE ROAD TO RIO 2012–2016

they had achieved. So I thought, how difficult could it be? Colin was at the top of his sport and was a clean-cut role model. Sadly here lays the problem. In Colin's case, he was just a judo player who loved his sport and came from an ordinary background.

To build his profile I searched the net and wrote to many media outlets to see if anyone was interested in Colin and I soon realised that a professional agent certainly earns their keep as I got nowhere. It was difficult to find contacts or any interest but then I suppose there was not much of a story to tell. An ordinary guy with no horrible history does not make good news.

But then I had an idea, primarily due to my brother Ralph, who had written many boxing articles and had interviewed many top-class boxers, like the great Howard Winstone, John Conteh and, my all-time favourite, Billy Walker, the blond heavyweight of the 60s who could pack any arena. I believed we could lift Colin slightly above the level of a judo player by bringing out a judo book. And so the process of writing a teaching manual judo book began in earnest. By December 2014 the book was completed and in the hands of a publisher. I have no doubts that the Commonwealth Games gold medal helped in getting us a contract.

At the beginning of 2015 Colin had a protracted injury that kept him out for nearly five months. It looked as if he would miss the European Championships to be held in Glasgow. Fortunately for us, but not so fortunate for British Judo, the championships were taken away from Britain by the European Judo Union after a dispute over sponsorship. It bought us time to get Colin fit and ready for the inaugural European Games, to be held in Baku, which now would double as the European Championships together with the Olympic ranking points. With so many points already on the board, it was still going to be hard for his rivals to catch him.

He returned to Baku where he reached the final of a Grand Slam for a third time and took some very welcome Olympic qualification points. It was to be the last medal he would take at an International Judo Federation tournament in the two-year Olympic cycle as his form dipped in and out. A seventh place at the World Masters yielded many points but in reality was just a solitary win; yes, against World silver medallist Sugoi Uriate, but nonetheless just one win. We timed the release of the *Getting Started* book to coincide with the European Games, in the hope of a big medal that would boost sales. Again, without wishing to labour the 'Rocky' ideal, had the script been written for a movie Colin would have taken a medal, the book would have boomed, and film contracts and TV offers would have rolled in. But no, Colin bombed out in the last 16 to Sergiu Oleinic.

The only consolation was that Colin had now represented his country at all the major Games: the Olympics, the European Games and the Commonwealth Games, a far cry from not even being considered for either the European Cadet Championships or the Youth Olympics in those early years. Nonetheless, the book did well even if we were not contacted by any film companies. I was concerned, however, that he had slipped over the hill.

He reached the final of the British Open at -73k on one of his better days, losing to Danny Williams. I could have been matside if I had wanted to pay the EJU for a coaching card but the parking fees at the venue required a bank loan so I decided to conserve my funds as the event (not being a qualification event) really did not matter at this stage of his career. Do not get me wrong, we wanted to win it, it is not in the Oates make-up to lose at anything, so I am not making any excuses for taking a second to Danny's fine performance on the day. Danny did the business in the professional way I would have expected. There was little chance of Colin's position in the world rankings being overtaken by any British rival as he was some 400-points ahead in the rankings and in a qualification spot. In my view Colin was spluttering to the Games. The internet trolls were quickly on the case yet again when someone posted 'Colin Oates is not capable of throwing anyone', a reference to the fact that most wins were now coming on the ground. The very fact that Colin was still ranked in the top eight of the world seemed to have gone unnoticed to this particular 'expert'. However, the climate had now changed and many came to Colin's defence on that post.

I too was often watching Colin on the live stream and wondering when and where the next throw was coming from or indeed what it might be. Over the past two years I had also realised that my basic training of Colin from an early age had been floored. There was no shock element in Colin's fight plan, so many top names could always, when the chips were down, produce something out of nowhere. In his early years we had almost perfected a brilliant wrong side shoulder throw which defeated a very talented opponent at a tournament in Peterborough but we had lost it over the years.

The problem being, if you are winning with the weapons you have in your armoury, why is there any need for anything in addition? With the internet there is no way of hiding a player – any elite athletes in all sports are likely to be the subject of coach scrutiny – so the answer must be that there is a need to constantly develop, regardless of your success. I often watched some of Colin's closer defeats and regretted so much we did not work more on that wrong shoulder technique. I realised too late for Colin that every player should have an emergency throw or two.

As we approached the European Championships I was becoming more and more concerned at Colin's form. Since recovering from his serious knee injury in 2015, it seemed even that fabulous groundwork was not so effective; this being said, the other possibility was that his opponents' coaches were more aware of what he was doing. With the winning on throws decreasing the groundwork was ever more vital. As already stated, with social media nowadays there is nowhere to hide and information on opponents is readily available.

I felt Colin was still spluttering in early 2016 but had taken a seventh place in Tokyo and had turned in a great performance losing the contest against World number two Tumurkhuleg Davaadorj on a couple of questionable penalties. However, some shock losses in Dusseldorf and Turkey did not suggest that Colin had much chance at what was possibly his last crack at the European Championships.

In Kazan, Russia, his draw was against the only man in the weight group older than him, 37-year-old Javier Delgado of

The final was an exciting contest between two great contestants.

The battle rages on.

A well-earned gold for Colin.

The customary parade and flag-waving ceremony.

A huge ovation from an appreciative Scottish crowd.

One of Kumo Judo Club's finest moments, boasting two members of the Rio Olympic squad on the stage at a Wolverhampton University dinner. Jonathan Drane is second left and Colin Oates third left.

Five-star prices for a room with a view in Rio in 2016.

Colin steps out into the arena as a Great Britain squad member, just minutes away from the end of a dream.

Denise unwinds after a traumatic week on Copacabana Beach in Rio.

Night-time on the beach in Rio.

Colin's homecoming attracted just over a handful of players, such was the price of a first-round Olympic exit.

Kumo Judo Club's finest as Colin and Jono warm up for a training session.

Colin takes a masterclass at Drake Judo Club in the west of England in 2016.

Another generation of the Oates family as Reece Oates competes at Breckland Leisure Centre.

Niamh and Eden Southgate celebrate double gold medals in Scotland in 2017.

The fighting Southgate sisters battle against each other in a final in Bredene, Belgium.

The back garden cabin still continues to provide a dojo facility for the club's players.

Spain. Some years earlier Delgado had defeated Colin at the British Senior Open, so it was a tricky opener which he won on a hold down. Colin's trusty groundwork came through again as he defeated Jasper Lefevere of Belgium and Fabio Basile of Italy (who just a few months later would take Olympic gold) before throwing Adrian Gomboc of Slovenia in a golden score semi-final to eventually lose to Vazha Margvelashvili of Georgia. The contest with Adrian Gomboc was a mammoth contest that seemed to last forever with Colin eventually winning in a fight to the finish golden score scenario. Gomboc would indeed become the European champion just a couple of years later such was his class. It was not just the fantastic silver medal that was vital but the Olympic qualification points that now opened the gap between him and his nearest British rival Nathon Burns to 600-points. It was now a mathematical impossibility for any British player to catch him. Our hopes were restored that Colin was back to his sparkling best.

Unfortunately, sometimes after a high in sport, there can be an immediate low, and another shock defeat in Baku at a Grand Slam brought us back to earth.

The top 16 ranking in the world qualified Colin for the World Masters in Mexico. We were at the time unsure whether there was any point in doing the event at all. However, finishing in the top 16 of the world is not easy and so the privilege of fighting in an event that was more difficult to qualify for than the Olympics meant there was little choice. Besides, Colin had never been to Mexico and I thought it may be nice to see where Corona lager comes from.

Colin made a first-round exit against Golan Pollack of Israel in a painfully close and tactical contest. It was now likely that Colin would confront the Olympics on the back end of three contest defeats in a row, not the best preparation for a major event. Looking at the officials and how they scored contests, I now seriously wondered if I understood the rules anymore.

Given Colin's groundwork skills, it only seemed fitting to release a book relating to that area of judo and our publishers were happy to go with it. We tried to time the release a month or so before the Rio Games and *Groundwork* was released in July 2016. By now, the intention was to pad Colin's income, as the UK Sport funding was not likely to last much beyond the Games and, with the future unclear, it was vital to have some independent funding backup.

There was now a lengthy preparation period for Colin's ultimate challenge and the trip was enormously expensive for Denise and myself, as could be expected. The host country, Brazil, and its residents and businesses were not likely to see an influx of foreign visitors in such numbers for some time to come so it was only to be expected we would be subjected to high prices and every conceivable other rip-off possible. Having booked our flights and hotels, to our horror Colin ripped tendons in his knee just weeks before the Games, putting in doubt whether he would even fight at the Olympics. When he rang me that night it was a deeply depressing conversation; we were not sure he would be fit for Rio. It meant he could not put in the same level of training or randori (sparring). It was not the best preparation although, it has to be said, I was not in favour of high levels of randori and

226

always believed the London team were beaten almost to death prior to those Games.

Before the departure came the customary 'Dinner Night' send-off at Wolverhampton University. This was going to involve eating a meal that you know will still leave you hungry whilst clad in something you have to wear that will leave you looking like an extra from a spy movie from the 1960s, all the while listening to some diatribe of speeches whilst trying to find something half-decent on your plate to eat. Well, to my surprise, it was a good meal and well presented; yes, I had to go out and buy a cheap suit from Matalan but was fortunate enough to have somehow thrown out my only pair of shoes some years back so could attend in my trainers, my only form of rebellion; however, on the whole, a good night, even if I did need to park half a mile away and have to walk the street in a suit. There were the customary speeches and, whilst not being one to look for praise, I thought it would have been classy to commend in some form the coaches that made that night happen, and in my case I did have two players on the stage, but no, it was not to be.

Colin and the team had departed much earlier than we did for Rio as Team GB made every effort to acclimatise all the athletes. This was not a trip either Denise or myself looked forward to and indeed, from the judo perspective, I did not think Colin's form was good either. The many years of making -66k were, in my view, clearly showing the strain, and the injury problem was clearly a hindrance.

As we approached the departure date Denise discovered we had not booked a room for the first night of our arrival and, upon forking out another 100 pounds for overpriced accommodation, realised that we had now double booked and were unable to cancel so, in addition to the ludicrous hotel price, we managed to pay twice for our first night. This was the Olympics and it is not too often you get to see a son compete at such an event so we swallowed the financial loss as you do.

We even booked a car and driver rather than depend on finding an honest taxi driver on arrival and I still think this was a prudent move. The flight of 11 hours was as you would expect – horrendous – the food was the usual airline stuff and did not look very inviting. In fact, the attendant missed giving me a tray but, on perusal of Denise's one, I decided not to make any complaint and just go hungry – it was the better option.

To our surprise many teams were also on the flight, including the Ukrainian judo team; I am sure none of their team had any trouble making their weight given the food on board. I did not appreciate how rich the UK is until finding out that many teams had to leave for Rio so late, clearly, I assumed, to meet a limited budget. Ukraine were engaged in a conflict with Russia at the time over the eastern area of the country including the Crimea so perhaps quite rightly they had other more important issues to spend money on.

Although Colin had trained and fought in Brazil many times, for Denise and myself it was the first time we had visited South America. I had done my research on the place and discovered that you could get drugs, women of the night and mugged anytime of the day, but the country that gave us the pleasure of Pelé had decided to ban casinos years earlier. You could not even get a game of bingo, perhaps not a bad thing. An 11-hour flight and no prospect of a game of blackjack was probably the last straw given the five-star hotel prices for back-street accommodation. Whilst it is true the car company that picked us up were brilliant, the hotel was less than ordinary. Our view was of a wall with graffiti in a language I had no chance of understanding. At least the hotel food was both palatable and relatively cheap. Unfortunately, whilst Rio may well be renowned for Copacabana Beach, the wine tasted as if it had been bottled directly from the ocean; I should have realised the wine problem by the absence of the French in the city who also love their wine. I still wonder where they stayed.

On arrival in Rio I was greeted by a text message from David telling me that Colin had another draw from hell; quite frankly, had I got the draw before boarding the flight from Schipol, we might well have flown back to Norwich. We had little expectation for Colin's chances as he had to get past two opponents he had previously lost to, but before then, he had to negotiate passage beyond Kilian Le Blouch of France, a player he had beaten a couple of times but only by a whisper.

To purchase our tickets we had to get to a shopping mall and to do that we needed something called a Rio card; this gave you access to the metro system. However, there was a catch; even with a Rio card you could only travel to the mall if you had a valid ticket to an event. The first problem was that, unfortunately, no one in Rio it appeared had any idea what a Rio card was. To be fair they only had some six years to prepare for the Games so perhaps the authorities could be forgiven.

Anyhow, Denise and I tried the tourist bureau who thought we wanted a credit card and on the week of the Games it was a bank holiday and all the banks were shut anyway. Just as well we had plenty of money. After some frantic street enquiries and no one having a clue what we were talking about or what language we were talking in we decided to go to a metro station.

A somewhat dingy building on a corner with the odd smashed window seemed to be a likely metro station but on entering I got a little suspicious we might be in the wrong place, by the very fact everyone in there seemed to be packing a gun. Well, this was Rio, so I still thought maybe this was not unusual for a metro. Amazingly it turned out to be the local police station and the language barrier was as evident here as it had been at the tourist board. There was much shouting and screaming at us and we genuinely thought we were about to be arrested as we were whisked up some dimly lit staircase and into a room that looked like it had seen many a waterboarding of a suspect. We were led to a lady police officer who spoke English and the whole sorry scenario was explained. Now, just when we were thinking the headline of the *Diss Express* was going to be 'Judo coach in custody in Rio', this lady took us under her wing and arranged a police escort to the real metro where we purchased our cards. The police were fantastic and seemed to have forgiven us for being somewhat stupid. To be fair, the metro station was not unlike the police station building; it was a mistake any idiot like me could have made.

That problem was resolved, we had our cards, but now we had to get to the mall and, even though there was a metro station there, we could not use that part of the line because we did not have the Olympic tickets which we could only get from the mall, a catch 22 situation. Hence a few nightmare journeys on a bus and eventually we jumped the queue, apparently because, as senior citizens, we could, and we were ready for the big day. My grey hair, something I had always blamed on Gareth Carder's many contests with Colin, had at least given me some advantage in life.

Many other sides of the draw looked much better than Colin's and, as usual at the Games, there were many shock exits; it meant a number of last-eight competitors were very unexpected. In many ways the very fact that, in my heart, I did not think Colin could make the last eight made it a little easier to swallow the controversial means by which Colin lost to Le Blouch. Colin had won both the previous meetings with the Frenchman but his last fight had been very close so I expected a tough contest. Indeed, any fight with a French player is always hard – they have such talent over the Channel.

The match was a tense affair and neither player looked capable of throwing the other. It was always likely to be won on penalties and with just 10 seconds on the clock Colin was leading by two penalties to one and on course for the next round when the referee surprisingly gave Colin a penalty for failing to attack just shortly after he attempted to throw Le Blouch. Victory was snatched from a tired Colin who was then presented with extra time. Both fighters commenced fighting with the scores even on penalties as Colin made a poor attempt at a sacrificial throw, drawing a third and decisive penalty from the referee. To say it was a gutting experience for all of us would be something of an understatement. If the next fight, to my mind, had been a relatively winnable match, I think I would have been devastated. The crowd booed Colin almost from the first attack and it has to be said there appeared to be a very hostile reception for him, so unlike London. I have to admit there was a sense of satisfaction when the home favourites were also eliminated; I know the crowd reaction cannot be laid upon an athlete but as a father I was hurt by the unexpected hostility, only human to react I guess.

Watching the young Italian Fabio Basile who Colin had beaten at the European Championships in Kazan just a few months earlier storm to the gold medal in sensational style probably rubbed salt in an already deep wound. Of course we did not resent the Italian's incredible performance that day but it does show the narrow margins between top flight players.

We met up briefly after the fight. What do you say to your son when his dream is shattered? Some 28 years of graft and sacrifice. Many still tell me he was a double Olympian but we eventually chased a bigger dream of a medal and got so very close. At 33 years old, we both knew, sitting in Rio, our long journey had all but come to the end; Tokyo was four years away, but may as well have been 20 years away.

I think the penny truly dropped a few days later when Colin Face Timed me from Rio after I had returned from Brazil. Here was an athlete who had dedicated the last 28 years of his life to a sport, unable to just retire and live in the country. In judo there are few, very few, who make any money, let alone enough to enjoy a comfortable lifestyle after they quit the sport.

At the Paralympics Kumo Judo Club's Jono Drane failed to lift that gloom, again so unluckily losing for a bronze against a fighter he too had defeated earlier in his career.

What followed on Colin's return was a meeting with British Judo and an assessment of how the year had gone, following which they would decide whether to put Colin forward for UK Sport funding or not. We were under no illusion – it was unlikely UK Sport would fund a 33-year-old athlete – and so when Colin was informed of the fact at the end of November we were hardly shocked.

My views were that I thought a common sense approach would be to fund him for a year on a player/coach basis so that the younger players could benefit from his presence on the mat at Walsall, but perhaps UK Sport did not have a box to tick for that scenario. As such, it was clear we had gone full circle and were now back to where we started at the beginning of the journey.

There were rumours Colin would be offered an 'athlete to coach' programme. The offer was apparently conditional upon Colin announcing his retirement, which created a chicken and egg situation. I was reluctant to advise him to retire in case the offer was not real but we were unsure if the offer could only be made once the retirement was announced. We were truly between a rock and a hard place. I was desperate to keep Colin in the public eye and not let him just fade into the mist.

The media, by which I refer to the local press, seemed more irate about Colin being cut from the programme and as such from any hope of UK Sport funding than we were. It is somewhat odd that, in the 21st century, when we are now so politically correct that any form of discrimination is rightly frowned upon, you could be considered too old for a particular function. I always thought British Judo might have been treading on eggshells by not putting him forward because of his age (not that any reason was ever given) which was probably why they announced two pathways to qualification for the Tokyo Games: the World Class Performance route, where everything was funded through UK Sport, and the self-funded route. Yes, now the Grands Prix and Continental Opens were on offer to all British squad players and, if you lifted yourself into the top 25 in the world, you could even self-fund a Grand Slam. Even your personal coach was now allowed to sit matside in the Grands Prix and below. We, indeed, did have the choice, if we genuinely believed Tokyo was a possibility for a 33-year-old; it just meant it was our money we had to use and not somebody else's.

There could be no argument that a player was blocked from qualifying for the Games on age, as an alternative route was now available, provided you could spare about 30,000 pounds a year.

Neither Colin nor myself ever felt bitter about the decision to drop him from funding and we could both see the logic of using the ever-decreasing UK Sport funding on younger stars, so we were never going to bite the hand of the very organisation that had kept us going for over ten years. Without the support of the British Judo Association we could never have achieved what we did.

Just before the British Trials in December came the announcement that Jonathan Drane was retiring and had no plans to engage on another four-year cycle at Walsall in a bid to qualify for the Games in Tokyo.

As we approached the British Championship I felt more nervous than I had been in Rio; whilst this was a much lower-level event, Colin was fighting at a much higher weight. In fact, in fighting in the under 81k section, he had effectively moved up two weight categories. Had I given the situation more thought the reality was that Colin, in fighting -66k, was always moving down a weight, so in the true sense Colin had only truly gone up one weight group, and with European Cup medals at -73k in the past, was this new weight asking that much? Well, for one thing, Colin was now heading towards his mid-thirties. Nonetheless, I still felt edgy, and being back matside for Colin, for the first time in two years, I felt the added responsibility to get him safely through the day.

Many watching that day would have been unaware that Colin had fought in Division Two of the Belgian League at -81k and so the weight was not that strange. The day was helped by the retirement of the brilliant Tom Reed and the unfortunate injury to the equally brilliant Stuart McWatt, two contests we were more than pleased we did not have to negotiate. That aside, we still had the British number one and Commonwealth Games gold medallist Owen Livesey to fight and a whole batch of other tasty young -81ks.

It turned out to be one of those days when everything went right and we managed to just pip Owen in a close final to take a fifth National Championship, leaving the question of where does the road lead to now? If you going to protest anything in sport, whether it be having your funding cut or non-selection for a major championship, it is always best to just get on with your sport and do your best rather than whine on and blame everyone but yourself. Colin, as always, answered on the mat. That day I was privileged to see my son fight just one more time at his brilliant best, the way he used to compete, and without the strains of making weight.

BEYOND RIO 2016–2020

IF THERE was any sense of satisfaction following the London Games, there was certainly no such feeling post-Rio. When I saw the first selections to the training camp in Austria in January 2017, it was a little heartbreaking after all these years not to see Colin's name on the list, the very fighter that had again bounced back from a disappointing result in Rio to win the British title, and the only possible reason being that he was now too old and time had run out. It was a little depressing.

It was Colin's desire to continue for another two years. Without funding and medical cover this was not going to be an easy pathway; however, we were not going to go down the road of travelling long distances to the easier Continental Cups in South America, Australia or Africa. Our attitude was to succeed or fail in tournaments that attracted the quality players and had the higher number of points attached to them. We had learnt from the experiences of other British athletes that those seeking to self-fund qualification needed success at Grands Prix to qualify for the Olympic Games, not that 2020 was ever our target. We were looking at one last crack at the Europeans and Worlds in 2018.

To achieve this goal would require meticulous planning and management. How amazing all those years ago I was said to be just a good manager; clearly, if there were to be any more miles on Colin's clock, management was essential.

Soon into 2017, if the non-selection for the Mittersill training camp made depressing reading, the selection for the Grand Slam in France left a more bitter taste; we really were on our own.

The problem (if it were a problem) Colin and I were presented with was the very fact we did not know how good Colin would be at -81k. Had a wonderful coaching position been offered to him early in 2017 it would have been a tough decision to make. Take a job in something he had dedicated his life to or test the 81k division at International level?

As it happened it was not a decision we had to make, so we had to look toward testing Europe. Somewhat ironic really, at a time when the UK was exiting Europe we were looking to go back into it. However, whatever we did now was going to be self-funded so Colin and I set ourselves a little target. We would target the European Championships in 2018 and our starting point would be back to where it all started, in Belgium. The Belgium Senior Open was the first major overseas International we ever attended, a place where I saw for the first time the standard of International judo. Not only was the standard high but each weight category attracted some 80–100 players. This event would be an ideal test and would provide a training camp for Colin too.

The Belgium Senior Open was indeed the first event we had to self-fund since the Grand Prix in Miami and Continental Open in San Salvador.

The cost was increased as Colin intended to stay on for the training camp that followed. I was unable to go with him as Denise was running the first-ever English Cadet Open at Thetford and my mat-laying skills were required. Colin was in safe hands as he was with the Scottish team and Euan Burton was the coach, a twice World medallist so hardly a guy that lacked judo experience.

The event was the usual monster with 58 players in Colin's new weight of -81k. Three wins saw Colin battle to the last eight but the two defeats that followed ended any medal hopes. I was able to see the two defeats on YouTube and my only thoughts were that he still had some way to go before he was truly in the weight category. We had at this stage half an eye on the back-to-back Continental Opens in Belarus and Romania in June but my gut feeling was to stick with the lower-level European Cups until we had developed into the weight properly – and there just happened to be one in Slovenia, also in June. The question of funding was still the main issue; I believed that Colin had a little more in his tank, but neither of us was prepared to invest huge amounts of money nor did we feel the need to effectively beg for money in pursuit of any of our dreams. That is not to say we shunned those that did, only that it was not our style.

I felt the camp in Belgium was good for Colin, not just because of the training; it made him still feel part of the International scene following the disappointment in Rio, and certainly the overall performance at an unforgiving tournament was pleasing. So many players hit downers following a career in sport and I was ever conscious of this.

On his return from Belgium, Colin announced on social media that he would take a break from competitions and get back in the gym; even though we had not had the discussion, he obviously felt, like me, that he was not truly in the weight category yet. The next date was the English Senior Open in April, an event that would not be as demanding as Belgium, and another opportunity to assess whether Colin should compete at a European Cup at an Open in June. My gut feeling was still the cup. The main aim of still fighting was to maintain Colin's competitive profile until something better came along. My efforts to get into more schools with money-making taster sessions were struggling and, with little or no support from local clubs at that time for any events I was promoting at my club, the road ahead was already looking rocky to say the least. So I needed to look at alternative ways to fund Colin's judo as I felt the masterclasses Colin was arranging should help his day-to-day needs.

The Grand Slam in Paris and the Grand Prix in Dusseldorf with their new world-ranking points allocations also confirmed that self-funding a European or Continental Open was tantamount to throwing money down the toilet if world ranking was your priority. The points now allocated to International Judo Federation events was disproportionate to those allocated to Continental Opens, where you could win six fights and earn 100-points, or just win a contest at a Grand Prix or Slam and get probably more points, especially if you were gifted with a bye and an automatic second-round contest. The bottom line being you could either win at this level or you could not. So we were fast coming to the conclusion that a self-funded Grand Prix may well be the last throw of the dice, but where?

Colin commenced his tour of masterclasses in March and he assisted at British Judo's Centre of Excellence. It was during his visit back to Lopham that he announced I should enter him for the English Senior Open at -73k as he could still make the weight. I was always unhappy with the desire to go to 81k which was why I wanted him to do the Belgium Open to prove a point. I had emphasised that, had I been in Belgium, I would have pulled him out of the repechage fight as his opponent looked so huge. The prospect of doing any further International events above the level of a European Cup at 81k was to my mind throwing money away. However, we were still looking at all options; now it was not just which Grand Prix but what weight too.

The announcement in April that the GB Team would fight at the European Championships was a further reminder of how difficult the road back would be to ever represent our country at the highest level, not to mention the expense. I had decided to plan well ahead and looked at the German European Cup and training camp in July as a possible way of keeping him in the frame. So a return to driving across Europe again loomed for me and we decided on entering my grandson Reece for a competition in Belgium in April, our first since 2013. As I suspected, the tournament was as difficult as they always had been, and Reece only ground out a bronze medal. Whilst the medal was not the colour I hoped for, it was an opportunity for me to get back into the mode of driving across Europe again and in many ways made me realise how much I had missed my visits to Belgium, the land of Jupiler beer. Moreover, the story of three generations of Oates family members fighting abroad was newsworthy and for the first time in some years we achieved good coverage in the local press with a story that only slightly was about Colin. I hoped the attention would keep the book sales ticking over.

The following week we returned to Walsall where Colin again fought -81k at the English Senior Open, much to my dismay as I would have preferred the -73k category. However, despite my reservations, Colin took gold beating Harry Lovell-Hewitt in the final, a win that catapulted him into the top four of the British rankings at the weight. Although the performance was flawless it did little to add substance to my argument that, if Colin was to do a major international again, the weight of -73k should be the target. He was showing less and less interest in the idea of making any challenge for a major selection and, looking at the financial implications, I had to agree the self-funding route was a daunting prospect, especially as masterclasses had saturated the judo circuit as every non-funded athlete looked to understandably support themselves. I believed Colin, who had always claimed in interviews that I would have been a millionaire had it not been for me funding his judo, had no intention of being a further drain on my resources.

As May arrived there seemed little on the horizon, judo job wise, and I was not too sure of the next steps to take to help him. Where does a judo player go when their career is almost at an end? Our family as a whole believed that Colin should set up his own business or even follow in the footsteps of his older brother and become a schoolteacher.

In May Colin returned to his roots and fought at Breckland Leisure Centre for the first time in six years and won five contests at -90k in the Anglian Team League and still looked in a different class. In less than 12 months Colin had descended from training camps and tournaments in Brazil, Russia and Mexico, to mention but a few, to competing at Walsall and Thetford.

Colin's decision not to fight at the European Open in Bucharest was looking like a good one as, with over 250 male entries, it would mean some five wins for a paltry amount of ranking points, whereas the Grand Prix in Mexico just a couple of weeks later was much lower in numbers and not that high a standard either which, in real terms, meant the single Grand Prix win was less work for much more. My aim was still to keep Colin's media profile very much alive and, despite my lack of expertise in that field, I was doing alright – we were still attracting local press coverage.

As we approached the halfway stage of 2017, it seemed less and less likely that Colin would fight in any further major International events. His training partner in Scotland, Gemma Gibbons, had called time on her wonderful career, and the prospect of Colin returning south would have meant, if not retiring completely, then at the very least giving up access to Ratho.

The Kumo Judo Club in Lopham had many years ago lost its classier players which would have meant Colin would have little in the way of training partners.

In June the International Judo Federation announced that Team Judo would make an appearance in the Tokyo Games but also revealed that Olympic qualification would be restricted to the top 18 of men and women. In real terms, with double-ups of nations, this meant you could still finish 21st in the world and, provided there were three or so Japanese above you, it was possible to secure qualification. However, there was that horrid knock-on effect that signalled the self-funded athlete's pathway was a little more difficult.

The good news from our perspective was that Colin was being asked to run club nights in Scotland and the masterclasses were still being booked. After some 12 years of sweating in front of a laptop watching Colin battle away at major events, it was nice to just watch the same events without the stress. The shortlist of the World selections for 2017 had a very different look and for the first time in ten years did not include Colin; there was an irony that he still was of that class but a part of me was relieved. Whilst Colin had silenced so many of his past keyboard warrior critics I was more concerned for his continuing reputation and I believed he may destroy his image if he went on too much longer at the higher level.

Many of Colin's contemporaries had either retired, pursued a self-funded pathway or had been given places at the Centre of Excellence; however, he never forgot the early support given to him by the Eastern Area and he represented his region by fighting once more for the senior team and nearly took them to a bronze medal. This, at present, is the last time Colin fought. The East only missed out on a countback of points. More to the point, he registered three fine wins at National level and kept his name in the sport picking up many more offers to perform masterclasses. The Eastern Area's senior examiner John Dearden made the long journey from Peterborough to Lopham Village Hall and Colin completed his 5th Dan theory at Lopham Village Hall with Jono Drane, who passed his 3rd Dan.

By July my attentions were drifting toward the future and I was unsure whether I even wanted to continue coaching anymore. I could have walked away and felt reasonably satisfied with what I had achieved. However, there were a number of players at the club beginning to show interest in competing again; I had acquired two very active girl players and the emergence of my grandson Reece all pointed to my return to travelling, back to Europe, effectively where we had developed Colin. The circle was close to joining together. In fact the circle was closing in other ways too as we learnt that British Judo had received an official complaint about our last inter-club competitions. Now there was originality – it was 1994 when we were first complained about and now in 2017 we are back where we started. Yes, there were still those out there with nothing better to do than complain. The complaint was largely ignored and we set about organising the next competition oblivious and quite apathetic to the identity of the anonymous figure behind the moan, just as we had been a couple of decades earlier.

Colin was now applying for jobs in British Judo and getting interviews. I still stood by the view that he should have followed in his brother David's footsteps and become a schoolteacher as indeed his former training partner Gemma Gibbons had, but it was his life and his pathway he had to pursue.

Then again, what does a parent know? My belief that Colin should draw a line under a judo career as a player was blown into orbit by his appointment as a junior elite support coach for the British squad; yes, the parent who advised his daughter against being a hairdresser who went on to run a thriving business was wrong again, and it seemed that all Colin had done was closed a chapter in his judo career whilst opening another.

It is a strange feeling to know that those early mornings watching your son and player fight in far-off lands would be no more. Those nerves, sometimes only pacified by drinking gallons of tea whilst wrapped in a blanket in front of your laptop watching Ippon TV, would be a distant memory. We had many trips across the world in the early days, sometimes not even knowing where the country was on the map. There were good times and bad times – sometimes, especially in the last 18 months before Rio when it was heartbreaking talking to Colin following a defeat, that perhaps should not have occurred, but that is sport.

There was no way we could end with the disappointment in Rio, which was why Colin fought in the British Championships in 2016 at two weights up at -81k. We needed and got that final special performance just one more time. Both of us always knew Tokyo 2020 was that one step beyond but it gave Colin something to focus on and that gold medal was as special as that first Junior Nationals medal we won back in 1995 when that nemesis of ours, Gareth Carder, spoilt our first final. At least I was in his chair that one last time, if not for his first National final debacle.

I never felt very involved in the period between 2013 and 2016 as Colin did not train at Kumo but, certainly up to 2012, when he took a European bronze, a World fifth and an Olympic seventh, he was most certainly training at Lopham Village Hall. It is clearly a reality that in the present climate the majority of personal coaches will lose their input as the Centre of Excellence takes control. However, with the high cost of travel and time consumption of training and fighting overseas almost every weekend, it is difficult to see how the average coach, who may well have a full-time job beyond judo, can commit so much time and money to this process. I was lucky to have been involved in the transition situation when the events were cheaper and you could stay in the budget hotels whilst attending the major Opens or training camps. I now see my role as a judo coach very differently to how I saw the situation back in the 90s.

We had a great journey and to say we did not achieve our dream would be very wrong because we did, many, many times over, but when we achieved one target we set another. When we set out, all we ever wanted as a family was my orange belt; as for Colin, we simply wanted a Junior Nationals bronze medal. Indeed, we were guilty constantly of moving those goalposts further and further back until they were just beyond our reach – that Olympic medal. In truth I never thought, back in my days of training at the Polytechnic of Central London in 1979, I would have a son that fought in one Olympic Games, let alone two; it was indeed accidental we went that far in the sport. Even more amazing to have had a player in Jono Drane who came so close to a Paralympic medal and all linked to that *Floodlight* magazine I purchased many years ago.

Colin finally announced his retirement from competitive judo on 18 September 2017, drawing an end to a long and successful career. He was appointed as support coach to the Great Britain junior squad on 1 October 2017.

He was back in the jet set travelling with his sport once more.

With the onset of the 2020 pandemic that led to the postponement of the Tokyo Olympics, we had certainly dodged a bullet by choosing the coaching course and not attempting to qualify as a self-funded athlete. Such qualification would have entailed more expense in attending the tournaments that were allowed to run for an Olympics in Japan that was by no means guaranteed.

Jono Drane came back out of retirement for the British Masters Championships held in Thetford in September 2018 and he claimed his first-ever National medal and was at last a British champion of some sort; it was my privilege to be in his chair one last time just like I had with Colin. That too was a fitting end to our wonderful partnership within this sport.

I returned with members of Kumo Judo Club to Belgium and my sister club Kemzeke for training and a competition weekend in 2018 as the cycle continued. Not quite as exciting as the travel Colin has to look forward to or where in fact I had been in the past 20 years but I have had my time. The arrival of the

Southgate family at my club, and in particular Eden and Niamh Southgate, gave me the inspiration to carry my dream on a little longer, that belief we could as a club still manage that elusive Olympic medal. I was about to draw back from the sport in 2017 and coach at recreational level, maybe even quit completely but it seemed any sense of fading from a scene I was never altogether comfortable with was lost, as within just six months of the sisters fighting for Kumo there was media interest in the Southgate sisters, which meant the inevitable appearances on radio and TV was likely to continue in the coming years.

In 2019 I commenced flying to events with my players again. I thought I had grown tired of the circuit, but it took a couple of sisters on my mat to make me realise that competitive judo is what I do and I cannot escape it. By the middle of the year I was jetting to Poland for Niamh Southgate's European Cadet Championship challenge where I planned to ghost in and out of the arena, but there was little chance of that and it was so nice to be told by the Great Britain squad managers that I had to sit with the team – this was such a classy gesture. And as recently as February 2020 I found myself in a Las Vegas hotel room nervously drinking cups of tea watching Niamh Southgate battling on Ippon TV at a European Cup in Spain. So much for saying goodbye to those tense mornings watching Colin. Even on holiday I do not seem to rest, knowing one of my fighters is competing somewhere.

I often asked myself the question, had all of my children quit judo in their teens would I have stayed in the sport? Had I walked away all those years ago, six of my grandchildren,

children of relationships within the sport, may never have existed and Christmas may have been a little less expensive. As a family we failed to get past the post on that Olympic medal but the sport of judo gave us much more and much better than that.

It has been my good fortune to be involved in elite judo since 2005 and I have met many players who it seems to me are very bitter about their failure to achieve the levels they thought they were capable of aspiring to. Often I find they claim it is someone else's fault – the governing body, the referees or a coach that failed them – when more probably it is simply the truth that the player did their best but just was not good enough. Many even attempt to rewrite history and tell a scenario that is simply far removed from the truth, a difficult task nowadays with most records easily available on the internet. Those who do not quite make it should be proud of what they achieved, anyone with the sheer guts to walk on an uncompromising judo mat with nowhere to hide should stand tall at whatever level they reached.

Yes, it would have been great to capture that Olympic or World medal, but Colin and I just did not quite make it and no one was to blame. It was not meant to be and there are no excuses, nor will there ever be, from Colin or myself. The whole journey was something of an accident anyway.

Colin continues his travels around the world as a coach and is as passionate as he ever was about his judo, and indeed I now travel again; we just do not travel together anymore. Time moves on.

Following Rio, I posted a quote on Kumo Judo Club's Facebook page, taken from John Lennon's last live gig with the

Beatles on the Apple rooftop in January 1969, and I make no apology for reiterating his words yet again: Thanks folks, I hope we passed the audition. We gave it our best shot and I hope those who followed us enjoyed the journey as much as we did and now have a greater understanding of what was truly involved.

Perhaps it is also now fitting to move on and mention Queen's last single release as more salient to the future: 'The Show Must Go On'.

RECORD OF MAJOR
COMPETITIONS

Record of achievement as a junior/youth (selected results only)

15/04/95 Bronze British Schools Championships, Cannock

21/10/95 Silver British Schools Championships Bradford

04/11/95 Silver British Junior Nationals, Crystal Palace

10/02/96 Silver BJA National Teams Championships,
          Crystal Palace

19/10/96 Gold British Schools Championships, Cannock

02/11/96 Gold British Junior Championships, Crystal Palace

01/11/97 Bronze British Junior Nationals, Crystal Palace

24/04/98 Gold British Schools Championships, Walsall

31/10/98 Bronze British Junior Nationals, Sheffield

13/04/99 Gold Liberty Bell Judo Classic, Philadelphia, USA

06/11/99 Bronze British Junior Nationals, Crystal Palace

09/04/00 Silver Liberty Bell Judo Classic, Philadelphia, USA

04/11/00 Gold British Junior Nationals, Crystal Palace

09/12/00 Gold VJF National Teams Div 3, Antwerp

10/11/01 Gold British Junior Nationals, Crystal Palace

25/11/01 Bronze British Youth Trials, Gateshead

24/03/02 Bronze Bremen International, Germany

05/10/02 Gold Welsh Senior Open, Cardiff

23/11/02 Gold British Junior Nationals, Willesden Record of achievement as a senior (selected results only)

24/11/02 Silver VJF National Teams Div 2 Antwerp

25/05/03 Gold Northern Irish Senior Open, Belfast

20/10/03 Gold Irish Senior Open, Dublin

13/12/03 Bronze British Senior Championships, Stoke-on-Trent

15/02/04 Gold London International, ExCel

07/03/04 Fifth New York Open, USA

21/03/04 Gold Ieper Senior Invitation, Belgium

23/05/04 Silver VJF National Teams, Antwerp

01/01/05 Gold Welsh Senior Open, Cardiff

13/02/05 Gold London International, ExCel

10/07/05 Bronze Turkish Open, Istanbul

03/12/05 Gold British Senior Open, Burgess Hill

18/06/06 Gold Commonwealth Tournament, Northern Ireland

14/10/06 Gold Genk Senior Invitation, Belgium

22/10/06 Gold Irish Senior Open, Dublin

03/12/06 Bronze British Senior Championship, Sheffield

08/04/07 Gold Lommel Senior International, Belgium

14/04/07 Bronze Swiss Open, Lucerne

26/05/07 Gold Northern Irish Senior Open, Belfast

04/11/07 Gold Swedish Open, Boras

10/11/07 Gold Finnish Open, Vantaa

02/12/07 Gold British Senior Championships, Sheffield

03/02/08 Bronze Belgium Open, Vise

04/05/08 Gold British Open, London

31/05/08 Gold Northern Irish Open, Belfast

20/09/08 Gold Continental Cup, Drammen, Norway

11/10/08 Bronze Irish Senior Open, Dublin

01/11/08 Silver British Senior Championships, Sheffield

09/11/08 Gold Finnish Open, Vantaa

22/03/09 Gold English Senior Open, Kendal

18/10/09 Bronze Scottish Open, Glasgow

01/11/09 Bronze Swedish Open, Boras

08/11/09 Bronze Finnish Open, Vantaa

31/01/10 Bronze Belgium Open, Vise

27/02/10 Bronze Continental Open, Prague

15/05/10 Bronze British Open, Burgess Hill

26/06/10 Silver European Cup, Orenburg, Russia

03/07/10 Fifth Grand Slam, Moscow

27/03/11 Gold English Senior Open, Sheffield

21/04/11 Bronze European Championships, Istanbul

23/07/11 Bronze European Cup, Hamburg

23/08/11 Fifth World Senior Championships, Paris

22/01/12 Gold British Senior Championships, Sheffield

04/02/12 Fifth Grand Slam, Paris

23/06/12 Bronze European Cup, Prague

29/07/12 Seventh Olympic Games, London

17/11/12 Silver Continental Cup, Apia

20/01/13 Silver British Senior Championships, Sheffield

22/06/13 Silver Continental Cup, San Salvador

20/07/13 Silver Grand Slam, Moscow

14/09/13 Bronze Grand Prix, Rijeka

19/10/13 Gold European Cup, Glasgow

15/12/13 Gold British Senior Championships, Sheffield

28/03/14 Bronze Grand Prix, Samsun

09/05/14 Gold Grand Slam, Baku

12/07/14 Seventh Grand Slam, Tyuman, Russia

24/07/14 Gold Commonwealth Games, Glasgow

27/11/14 Bronze Grand Prix, Jeju, Korea

8/05/15 Silver Grand Slam, Baku

23/05/15 Seventh World Masters, Rabat

11/07/15 Silver British Senior Open, London

18/07/15 Seventh Grand Slam, Tyumen, Russia

4/12/15 Seventh Grand Slam, Tokyo

19/02/16 Seventh Grand Prix, Dusseldorf

21/04/16 Silver European Championships, Kazan, Russia

8/12/16 Gold British Championships (first event at
      -81k), Sheffield

29/04/17 Gold English Senior Open, Sheffield